First World War
and Army of Occupation
War Diary
France, Belgium and Germany

25 DIVISION
Divisional Troops
111 Brigade Royal Field Artillery
15 September 1915 - 27 November 1916

WO95/2233/4

The Naval & Military Press Ltd
www.nmarchive.com
Published in association with The National Archives

Published by

The Naval & Military Press Ltd

Unit 10 Ridgewood Industrial Park,

Uckfield, East Sussex,

TN22 5QE England

Tel: +44 (0) 1825 749494

www.naval-military-press.com

www.nmarchive.com

This diary has been reprinted in facsimile from the original. Any imperfections are inevitably reproduced and the quality may fall short of modern type and cartographic standards.

© **Crown Copyright**
Images reproduced by permission of The National Archives, London, England, 2015.

Contents

Document type	Place/Title	Date From	Date To
Heading	WO95/2233/4		
Heading	111th Brigade R.F.A. Sep 1915-Nov 1916		
Heading	25th Division 111th Brigade R.F.A. Vol I Sept 15 15-Nov		
War Diary	Aldershot	15/09/1915	25/09/1915
War Diary	Southampton	25/09/1915	25/09/1915
War Diary	Havre	26/09/1915	26/09/1915
War Diary	Caestre	27/09/1915	27/09/1915
War Diary	Oosthove Farm	28/09/1915	30/09/1915
Heading	25th Division 11th Bde. R.F.A. Vol 2 Oct 15.		
War Diary	Ploegsteert	01/10/1915	31/10/1915
Heading	25th Division 111th. Bde. R.F.A. Vol. 3		
War Diary	Near Ploegsteert In Green Portions	01/11/1915	23/11/1915
War Diary	Near Ploegsteert	24/11/1915	30/11/1915
Heading	25th Division 111th. Bde. R.F.A. Vol. 4 Dec 15		
War Diary	In Gene Positions Nr. Ploegsteert.	01/12/1915	31/12/1915
Heading	111th. Brigade R.F.A. 25th. Divisional Artillery January 1916.		
War Diary	In Positions Near Ploegsteert	01/01/1916	31/01/1916
Heading	111th. Brigade R.F.A. 25th. Divisional Artillery February 1916.		
War Diary	Caestre	01/02/1916	03/02/1916
War Diary	Bollezeele	04/02/1916	13/02/1916
War Diary	Bollezeele To Caestre	14/02/1916	14/02/1916
War Diary	Caestre	15/02/1916	29/02/1916
Heading	111th. Brigade R.F.A. 25th. Divisional Artillery March 1916.		
War Diary	Caestre	01/03/1916	09/03/1916
War Diary	Mazinghem	10/03/1916	10/03/1916
War Diary	Boyaval	11/03/1916	16/03/1916
War Diary	Orlincourt	17/03/1916	31/03/1916
Heading	111th. Brigade R.F.A. 25th. Divisional Artillery April 1916.		
War Diary	Orlencourt And Monchy	01/04/1916	01/04/1916
War Diary	Breton (In West Billets)	02/04/1916	20/04/1916
War Diary	Orlencourt (In West Billets)	22/04/1916	23/04/1916
War Diary	Guns In Position In Geeu Pits W & S.W of Neuville	24/04/1916	24/04/1916
War Diary	St Vaast	25/04/1916	30/04/1916
Heading	111th. Brigade R.F.A. 25th. Divisional Artillery May 1916.		
War Diary	In Gene Positions W Of Neville St Vaast	01/05/1916	21/05/1916
War Diary	Guns At ACQ Except. A Battery Still In Action	22/05/1916	25/05/1916
War Diary	In Action	26/05/1916	29/05/1916
War Diary	Guns Less 2 Sections In Action S.W of Neuville St Vaast.	30/05/1916	31/05/1916
Heading	111th. Brigade R.F.A. 25th. Divisional Artillery June 1916.		
Miscellaneous	3rd. Echelon. Base.	01/07/1916	01/07/1916
War Diary	Roellecourt	01/06/1916	01/06/1916
War Diary	Battery. & H-Qs.	02/06/1916	02/06/1916

War Diary	Batteries In Action	03/06/1916	03/06/1916
War Diary	Under 51st Div-Near Neuville St Vaast	04/06/1916	15/06/1916
War Diary	Outrebois	16/06/1916	17/06/1916
War Diary	Fieffes	18/06/1916	26/06/1916
War Diary	Fieffes (In Reserve)	27/06/1916	27/06/1916
War Diary	Contay (In Reserve)	28/06/1916	30/06/1916
Heading	Headquarters. 111th Brigade, R.F.A. July 1916		
War Diary	Contay	01/07/1916	05/07/1916
War Diary	In Action In The Open S.E Of Bouzincourt	06/07/1916	06/07/1916
War Diary	In Action S.E of Bouzincourt	07/07/1916	11/07/1916
War Diary	In Juee Positions W 18b X W 18d W 12d.	12/07/1916	18/07/1916
War Diary	In Action As Before	19/07/1916	31/07/1916
Heading	111th Brigade. Royal Fieldartillery August 1916		
Miscellaneous	Staff Captain 25th D.W. R.A.	31/08/1916	31/08/1916
War Diary	Guns In Action W Of Ovillers	01/08/1916	05/08/1916
War Diary	Guns In Actions As Before.	06/08/1916	24/08/1916
War Diary	In action as before	25/08/1916	31/08/1916
Operation(al) Order(s)	25th Divisional Artillery Operation Order No. 42. Appendix 1	03/08/1916	03/08/1916
Operation(al) Order(s)	25th Divisional Artillery Operation Order No. 43. Appendix 2		
Miscellaneous			
Operation(al) Order(s)	25th Divisional Artillery Operation Order No. 44. Appendix 3	08/08/1916	08/08/1916
Operation(al) Order(s)	25th Divisional Artillery Operation Order No. 45. Appendix 4	09/08/1916	09/08/1916
Operation(al) Order(s)	25th Divisional Artillery Operation Order No. 46. Appendix 5	12/08/1916	12/08/1916
Miscellaneous	Time Table For 18 Pdr. Guns. 25th Divisional Artillery. Night August		
Miscellaneous	Time Table for 4.5th Hows. 25th Divisional Artillery.		
Operation(al) Order(s)	25th Divisional Artillery Operation Order No. 47. Appendix 6	14/08/1916	14/08/1916
Miscellaneous	Time Table 25th Divisional Artillery		
Heading	111th. Brigade R.F.A. 25th. Divisional Artillery September 1916.		
Miscellaneous	Staff Captain 25th Div		
War Diary	In Action S.W Of Ovillers	01/09/1916	08/09/1916
War Diary	As Before but Not In Action	09/09/1916	28/09/1916
War Diary	In Position In R32 C.	29/09/1916	30/09/1916
Heading	111th Brigade R.F.A. 25th. Divisional Artillery October 1916.		
War Diary	In Action Between Pozieres And Ovillers Gesses In Action	01/10/1916	07/10/1916
War Diary	Between Pozieres & Ovillers	08/10/1916	25/10/1916
War Diary	For The Field North Of Pozieres By Mouquet Farm (Gens In Action)	26/10/1916	31/10/1916
Heading	111th. Brigade R.F.A. 25th. Divisional Artillery November 1916.		
War Diary	Guns In Action Close to Mouquet Farm On East Side.	01/11/1916	21/11/1916
War Diary	Guns In Action Close Action Albert	22/11/1916	22/11/1916
War Diary	In The Road To Near Area.	23/11/1916	27/11/1916

10/9/22/4

25TH DIVISION
DIVL ARTILLERY

111TH BRIGADE R.F.A.
SEP 1915 - NOV 1916

BROKEN UP

12/6991

25th Division

III Brigade R.F.A.
Vol: I

Sept. 1. 15
Nov. 16

Vol I

Instructions regarding War Diaries and Intelligence Summaries are contained in F. S. Regs., Part II. and the Staff Manual respectively. Title pages will be prepared in manuscript.

WAR DIARY

~~INTELLIGENCE SUMMARY.~~

(Erase heading not required.)

Army Form C. 2118.

Place	Date	Hour	Summary of Events and Information	Remarks and references to Appendices
ALDERSHOT	Sept Night 24th-25th	–	Brigade entrained during this night and finished entraining at 9-20 a.m. 25th Sept '15. Weather fine.	R.A.
SOUTHAMPTON	25th	a.m. 11 to 1 p.	Detrained at SOUTHAMPTON. Embarked during afternoon for HAVRE. Good passage – Fine.	R.A.
HAVRE	26th	10-30 A.M.	Arrived HAVRE by 10-30 a.m. Disembarked. Remained at HAVRE till the evening – entrained at various hours during the night.	R.A.
CAESTRE	27th	10 A.M.	In the train – Batteries detrained at CAESTRE. Billeted 3 Batteries and Brigade Amm. Col. at PRADELLES and Head Quarters and "A" Battery at VIEUX BERQUIN – Remained the night there.	R.A.
DOSTHOVE FARM	28th	9 A.M. 6 p.m.	Received orders at 9 A.M. to move into position near PLOEGSTEERT. This was done at dusk, taking over line previously held by 64th Brigade R.F.A. of 12th Division. Brigade Head Qrs. billeted at DOSTHOVE FARM. Batteries in position near PLOEGSTEERT.	R.A.
	29th		Batteries check registration taken over. Weather very wet – condition of roads very bad.	R.A.
	30th		Continue registration. "B" Battery retaliated on a German Battery which was shelling our trenches, and the Battery stopped firing	R.A.

NOTE: All places referred to from 28/9/15 inclusive Reference Maps 1/20000 Belgium 28 S.W.

D/
7431

35th Division

111th Bde: R.F.A.
Vol 2

Oct 15.

111th Brigade R.F.A.

Army Form C. 2118.

WAR DIARY
INTELLIGENCE SUMMARY.
(Erase heading not required.)

Instructions regarding War Diaries and Intelligence Summaries are contained in F.S. Regs., Part II. and the Staff Manual respectively. Title pages will be prepared in manuscript.

Place	Date	Hour	Summary of Events and Information	Remarks and references to Appendices
PLOEGSTEERT	1.10.15	3.30 p.m.	A Battery registered on a new zone it having been changed to cover fresh trenches (N°s 110, 111, 112) The other Batteries continued Registration of various targets. 2C	
"	2.10.15	2.45 p.m. to 3.45 p.m.	Batteries continued Registration during the day. The enemy shelled PLOEGSTEERT CHURCH on and off between 2.45 p.m. & 3.45 p.m. A few of the shells fell near A Battery's Position. Other Batteries registered. 2C	
"	3.10.15	11.30 a.m.	The enemy's artillery was not active on our front. The forward in V.27.6.8.3 behind French 107. were at 7.35 c.m. The enemy shelled. 3/111 Registered a zero line. There was no retaliation by the gun. 6 or 7 shells were fired - enemy. A German Observation Balloon was observed up in the morning & returning 2C	
	4.10.15	6.15 a.m. 3.30 p.m.	A few German Howitzer Shell fell in PLOEGSTEERT. A large German double-engine fighting Plane was observed over our Trenches. It went North, dropping a smoke bomb, and then disappeared in the clouds near ARMENTIERES. The German Observation Balloon was up during the day. 2C	
	5.10.15	1.30 p.m.	B. Battery fired during the day on the enemy's Trenches at a Range of 3800 x with corrector 120. The burst appeared to be effective. A White flag was observed waving in the German Trenches. Bearing from LONDON FARM 78° Mag. A fairly quiet day - Very wet, & ground very muddy - 2C	
	6.10.15		Nothing of importance to report. A fine day but misty in the morning 2C	
	7.10.15	10.30 a.m.	A German working party was observed moving about near a hut at O.22.d.1.4. The enemy may have an Observation Post there as 2 Telephone wires were plainly visible - Fire was opened on the hut at 10.30 a.m & a direct hit obtained 2C	
	8.10.15		Nothing of importance occurred - 2C	
	9.10.15		Very misty day & bad for Observation. A Machine Gun Emplacement in the BIRDCAGE was hit by D Battery but with little effect as the place is very strong (Revetted) 2C	

2353 Wt. W2544/1.54 700,000 5/15 D.D. & L. A.D.S.S./Forms/C. 2118.

Army Form C. 2118.

WAR DIARY

INTELLIGENCE SUMMARY.

(Erase heading not required.)

Instructions regarding War Diaries and Intelligence Summaries are contained in F.S. Regs., Part II. and the Staff Manual respectively. Title pages will be prepared in manuscript.

Place	Date	Hour	Summary of Events and Information	Remarks and references to Appendices
PLOEGSTEERT	10/10/15	2 p.m.	A working party was visible near a hut at U.22.d.2.4 who appeared to be pumping water. A few rounds fired by A Battery dispersed the party. A 77 cm Battery was reported to have been located at SOMMER FARM U.29.c.3.5. This was fired on by B Battery but it is not known if any damage was done. A Working Party which had been previously reported working on an emplacement in V.21.b.8.1 did not resume work last night. &c	
	11/10/15	5.15 a.m.	The above working party was again observed, but was dispersed by Rifle Fire. The enemy wore no caps. During the night a German Patrol (some within 20 yds of Trench 119 and left a piece of paper stuck in the shape of an Eagle. The Trenches opposite 119-120 are reported to be well manned as a large volume of Rifle Fire was brought to bear from time to day on our Aeroplanes. &c	
	12/10/15		A very quiet day on our front. A light had been seen last night in Farm buildings in V.22.d.2.2. An Observation Station is suspected there. A Battery shelled these buildings during to day but the damage, if any, is not known &c	
	13/10/15	2 p.m.	The 28th Division carried out to day a Demonstration in connection with other parts of the front. The 11th Brigade took part in the Demonstration which consisted in wire cutting & destruction of enemy's parapets between points (C.11.c.1.9) & (C.10.b.4.3). B Battery was allotted stations on	
		16	the task of shelling Trenches opposite Trenches 94 & 95. (C.10.b.5.7 & C.4a.2.f) with H.E. SHELL. This Battery succeeded probably damaging their parapets. The Battery fired 150 H.E. SHELL.	
		5 p.m.	During the operations a single Gun D Battery at ESSEX FARM (D.28 & 9.6) which was replacing Trenches S of LE TOUQUET was located by the enemy and heavily shelled with 7.7 cm & 15 cm Shell. Fortunately no damage was done. Troops shells fell all round the gun, one falling within 5 yards of it. This gun was withdrawn during the night. This gun was in charge of Sergt PARTON who is about to proceed to ENGLAND on being commissioned as a 2nd Lieut. The other Batteries kept up a consistant fire on the enemy's Trenches in front of them. Very little Ammunition being distributed &c. Our rifle fire on the enemy's parapet was difficult. &c	

Army Form C. 2118.

WAR DIARY
INTELLIGENCE SUMMARY.
(Erase heading not required.)

Instructions regarding War Diaries and Intelligence Summaries are contained in F. S. Regs., Part II. and the Staff Manual respectively. Title pages will be prepared in manuscript.

Place	Date	Hour	Summary of Events and Information	Remarks and references to Appendices
PLOEGSTEERT	14/10/15		A very quiet day — Nothing of importance occurred.	2C
	15/10/15		A very quiet day — A sniper's emplacement opp- to trench 102 had particular attention given to it by B. Battery which put a few direct hits on it — Nothing else to report.	2C
	16/10/15	9. a.m.	The Sniper's Post referred to yesterday was made untenable by B. Battery.	2C
		3.30 p.m.	A suspected Observation Station was shelled by A Battery & a portion of the Hop was seen to collapse.	2C
	17/10/15		A very quiet day. Nothing to report.	2C
	18/10/15		The enemy's artillery was rather more active to-day. The firing appeared to come from AV.GHEER. Observing Station was shelled to-day but not actually hit. The direction of PONT ROUGE. The O.C. B Battery reports a good day's work firing on behind Trench 102. Probable cause to decrease. Shine by our shell fire a few rounds of "D" battery at the report the infantry shelled a 77 c.m. gun located at V.21.6.6.4. Hewill fire no further trouble.	2C
		2.40	A good many 150 m.m. H.E. shell fell in the vicinity of C. 13 battery's position. This was evidently	2C
			unobserved fire & the battery does not appear to have been located.	
	19/10/15		A church in PONT ROUGE which is clearly visible from the O.P. at LONDON. FARM seems to be used Observation Station — The Church is at V.29.6.4.7. B. Battery is reported the following information	2C
	20/10/15	9.30 a.m.	B. Battery observed a working party opposite Trench 104 and did some damage to the enemy's	2C
		3.45 p.m.	Parapet still. It is hoped work there will now be abandoned. A fortress at V.16 C.8.0 also appeared to do some damage to it.	2C
	21/10/15		Nothing to report. Very misty in the morning.	2C
	22/10/15	3.30 p.m.	Again very misty. D Battery destroyed a good work to-day. A working party a V.21.6.6.3 was fired at and the Parapet where they were working damaged. The working party returned to work at 10 p.m. but were dispersed by fire from D Battery. This battery also observed a light Trench Railway at V.21.6.9.4 & opened fire = of all a bit & destroyed part of the line & one Truck.	2C

2353 Wt. W2544/#154 700,000 5/15 D. D. & L. A.D.S.S./Forms/C. 2118.

Army Form C. 2118.

Instructions regarding War Diaries and Intelligence Summaries are contained in F. S. Regs., Part II. and the Staff Manual respectively. Title pages will be prepared in manuscript.

WAR DIARY
INTELLIGENCE SUMMARY.
(Erase heading not required.)

Place	Date	Hour	Summary of Events and Information	Remarks and references to Appendices
PLOEGSTEERT	25/10/15	2.45 to 4 p.m	The enemy put a few shells into PLOEGSTEERT – This was probably done in retaliation for the shelling of LA PETITE HAIE FARM (V.23.d.9.9) by "A" Battery who obtained at least one direct hit on it. – Some works going on in the BIRDCAGE were damaged by "D" Battery.	2C
	24/10/15		An unusually quiet day – Nothing to report.	
	25/10/15	11.p.m & 11.30/and	A very wet day – Observation practically impossible. – The enemy at 11 p.m. threw phosphorous into our trenches. – A salvo at 11 p.m. & another at 11.30 p.m. in practice from fired by "C" Battery on to the enemy's trenches put a stop to this.	2C
	26/10/15		The enemy's Artillery was very fairly quiet & the weather unimproved. One of the best days for light in a long time.	2C
	"	10.45 a.m.	A Sniper's post in a tree opposite Trench 103 was fired at by B Battery. The Tree was shattered. Two Germans were observed by a man of "D" Battery to be in a ruined house between the trenches (V.21.6.6.3) They were fired at by the S.m of the XI Cheshires several times. but they always ducked & then signalled "Wash. Out". They were dressed in blue & wore blue hats with red bands and a metal design in the centre.	
	"	3.15 p.m.	LIEUT. HIGGS a forward observing officer observed for some time from Trench 120 a man on one working from behind a mound on the left of the "BIRDCAGE". The puffs of smoke were very regular and probably came from the Vertical Boiler type – This mound has been shelled several times and has invariably brought retaliation on us, which may prove that the enemy have something of value behind it.	2C
	27/10/15		A very quiet day – A detachment of 20 men under Lieut BAKER represented the Brigade at an inspection by His Majesty The King.	2C
	28/10/15		Nothing to report. A very wet windy day.	2C
	29/10/15		Nothing of importance occurred, except that an unfortunate accident occurred, through the explosion of a Yellow Fume – whistle killed a man of "B" Battery who was examining it	2C

Army Form C. 2118.

WAR DIARY
INTELLIGENCE SUMMARY.
(Erase heading not required.)

Instructions regarding War Diaries and Intelligence Summaries are contained in F. S. Regs., Part II, and the Staff Manual respectively. Title pages will be prepared in manuscript.

Place	Date	Hour	Summary of Events and Information	Remarks and references to Appendices
PLOEGSTEERT	30/10/15	10 a.m. to 12 noon	A much finer day. The German Artillery was more active and "D" Battery's O.P. at ST YVES came in for a good deal of shelling. The Battery retaliated on the BIRDCAGE. 2©	
	31/10/15		A dirty wet day. AV GAFER the O.P. of "A" Battery came in for more shelling but there will no casualties. 2©	

III/ Bat. 18 Pa.
Vol. 3

12/7635

25th Division

9 Nov 15.

111th Brigade R.F.A.
according to no

Army Form C. 2118

WAR DIARY
or
INTELLIGENCE SUMMARY
(Erase heading not required.)

Instructions regarding War Diaries and Intelligence Summaries are contained in F.S. Regs., Part II. and the Staff Manual respectively. Title pages will be prepared in manuscript.

Place	Date	Hour	Summary of Events and Information	Remarks and references to Appendices
Near PLOEGSTEERT in our Positions	1.11.15		A very wet and unusually quiet day. AUGHER was again shelled by the enemy	
	"	4.15pm	Support Trenches behind Trench 120 were also shelled, but this was effectively put a stop to by Retaliation on the BIRDCAGE by "D" Battery. SC	
	2.11.15		Another very wet and quiet day. The enemy was being worked on his front line trench in the BIRDCAGE	
	3.11.15		An improvement in the weather, but both sides were fully employed in repairing SC trenches damaged by rain.	
	"	11 a.m.	A few shell were again fired into the vicinity of AUGHER & a few "Minen bangs" came from the direction of LE TOUQUET. Our fire was protracted 6. Day to enable our infantry to repair their trenches – "D" Battery fired about 4 p.m. and some working parties reported by the Infantry SC	
	4.11.15		The Infantry reported that the firing by "D" Battery the night before was very effective. An explosion was caused in the German Trench & flares were distinctly heard. Two direct hits were obtained this morning by "B" Battery on a suspected Observation Station V.28.d.2.2½ A very quiet day – SC	
	5.11.15	9.45 am	A Bringe HE was observed by an aeroplane Sentry from "B" Battery – It appeared to be almost stationary and was being shelled when observed.	
		1.34 pm	×This 13 atery observed 2 aircrafts on a Ferman Howitzers at V.30.c.0.8 suspected on 13th Oct. SC	
		2.15 pm	obtained 3 direct hits on a Ferman suspected being an observation station (O.5.b.4.5)	
		3 pm	"B" Battery also registered a tall Chimney at V.30.d.4.2 which has an erection on it top of it & is suspected of being and Observation Station. SC	
	6.11.15		A very foggy day – nothing to report. SC	
	7.11.15		Another very foggy day – Nothing to report - SC	

Army Form C. 2118

WAR DIARY
or
INTELLIGENCE SUMMARY.
(Erase heading not required.)

Instructions regarding War Diaries and Intelligence Summaries are contained in F. S. Regs., Part II. and the Staff Manual respectively. Title pages will be prepared in manuscript.

Place	Date	Hour	Summary of Events and Information	Remarks and references to Appendices
Near PLOEGSTEERT in your Poilous	8.11.15		The enemy's Artillery was more active to-day. During the day the enemy fired about 20-25 Shells in rear of the junction of our Trenches 10/10/2 C.4.a.4.7. Retaliation on the enemy's trenches by "B" Battery appeared to be effective. It seems almost certain now that the tall chimney at V.30.d.4.2 is used as an observation position. Infantry Officers report having seen figures & movement by means of a powerful telescope. 2C	
	9.11.15 10.15 p.m.		PLOEGSTEERT was shelled but "D" Battery put a stop to this by shelling DEVERMONT Retaliation on this place generally appears to be effective	
		2.50 p.m.	A canvas screen 50 yds x 20 ft was observed by "B" Battery at V.28.d.4.7 - Ran Battery fired at it but did not damage it apparently to see what was behind it. The spot is being carefully watched. 2C	
	10.11.15 4.10 p.m.		PLOEGSTEERT again shelled. Retaliation by "D" Battery on DEVERMONT was again effective. LIEUT BAKER of "B" Battery picked up 2 flashes from the gun which is shelling "B" being at C.6.b.3.2. The railway screen reported yesterday was again visible. It may be a "Snare" but it may be covering the digging of a new communication trench. C/o the area near V.28.d.4.8. is becoming rather "chewed up." "A" Boarding" has been showing for some days at the Northern mound of the BIRD CAGE. This was removed to-day and a brief construction has come to light. It is so conspicuous that it is probably only meant to draw fire. 2C	
	11.11.15		A quiet day - poor light in the morning. "B" Battery registered at Road Junction V.30.c.6.7. Two Cyclist Orderlies, 2 Transport Wagons & several individuals were seen in that neighborhood.	

Army Form C. 2118.

WAR DIARY
or
INTELLIGENCE SUMMARY.
(Erase heading not required.)

Instructions regarding War Diaries and Intelligence Summaries are contained in F. S. Regs., Part II. and the Staff Manual respectively. Title pages will be prepared in manuscript.

Place	Date	Hour	Summary of Events and Information	Remarks and references to Appendices
Nor. ROEGSTEERT in Gun Positions	11.11.15 (Tm)	1.15 p.m.	Shortly after the registration individuals were seen dashing about at great speed in some cases the "crouching" attitude was adopted. A German mounted the steps in his trench & surveyed the country for about 30 secs. This was opposite the junction of our trenches 102/103 – He was dressed in the usual grey tunic with a thin line of red round it. He appeared to be dirty & unkempt but otherwise prosperous & self-satisfied. "B" Battery reports these were in front of Trenches 104 × 105 – to have been laid in a haphazard way.	
		12.25 p.m.	Parties of the enemy seen coming & going in the direction of the Rich were scared by the shooting of "H" Battery. SC	
	12.11.15	6.p.m	A very wet & stormy day – PLOEGSTEERT was shelled at 6p.m – One of the shells burst in the kitchen of the "C" Battery Officers billet. Capt. KERANS the B.C. was struck & had a narrow escape. SC	
	13.11.15		Another very dreary wet morning – Nothing to report. SC	
	14.11.15		A fine day & pretty. Capt. KERANS had another escape a shell falling close to his telephone dug-out – he was struck in the wrist. 2nd Lieut. T. JOMARON is attached for training from RAC to D Battery SC	
	15.11.15	9.p.m	Some 4.2 c.m. Shell fell close to D Battery's Wagon Lines - These were undoubtedly fired with a view to knocking out one of our Heavy Guns in action nearly. SC	
	16.11.15		Very misty day - Only 1 Round fired all day by the Batteries of this Brigade SC	
	17.11.15	1.15 p.m.	GOSTHOVE FARM. my H.5.2 was shelled – fortunately no casualties though there were several so 40yds away while the PIONEER 13th BATTALION (S.W. 73) au Billeted – B. Battery successfully retaliated on the enemy's Trenches – Other useful work was done by my Batteries in knocking parties SC	

WAR DIARY
or
INTELLIGENCE SUMMARY.

Army Form C. 2118.

Instructions regarding War Diaries and Intelligence Summaries are contained in F.S. Regs., Part II. and the Staff Manual respectively. Title pages will be prepared in manuscript.

(Erase heading not required.)

Place	Date	Hour	Summary of Events and Information	Remarks and references to Appendices
Near PLOEGSTEERT in gun Positions	18.11.15	3 p.m.	Light was bad to-day & observation difficult - S'YVES received some attention from German Shells & PLOEGSTEERT was shelled as usual & the usual retaliation on DEVIL'S WOOD (and) only by "D" Battery - Various "mounds" are appearing in the German Parapets - Rose in my zone we being dealt with. ZC	
	19.11.15		The Enemy's Artillery was inactive to-day. 'C' Battery engaged some fresh loopholes at U. 23.a.1.2. & "mounds" were again shelled by my Battery. ZC	
	20.11.15	3.30 p.m	The enemy's Artillery was fairly quiet - 'C' Battery (V. 25.c.2.3) - A fuze picked up two shells fell close to the gun position. 'A' Battery damaged one of the "mounds" at here was thought to be a French fuze -	
		4.30 p.m	V. 20.a.5.8 with H.E. Shell. WOODMAN went out & reconnoitred	
		8 p.m	the enemy's barbed wire opposite AD CHEER - He could not get right opposite the "mound" at V. 25.a.5.8. on account of German Sentries. He reports the wire as very strong & that some of the knife rests are 9' iron. ZC	
	21.11.15		The enemy's Artillery was singularly inactive - A fine day. Frost at night. Re "Mound" at V. 21.c.6½.4 was a good bit knocked about by "D" Battery. During the night LIEUT. WOODMAN of 'A' Battery again went out & reconnoitred in front of our trenches. ZC	
	22.11.15		Nothing much going on - Very foggy - and "reliefs" of Infantry taking place - There two factors stopped 2nd Battery going. ZC	
	23.11.15	3.30 p.m	The Enemy's Artillery was quiet to-day - A probable Machine gun Emplacement at U.28.a.5.7 and a "mound" at U.21.b.6½.4 were respectively bombarded by 'A' & "D" Batteries and a good deal of damage done - One gun of "D" Battery which was in the Wagon line was moved to ESSEX FARM in the night & prepared to support Trenches S.9 LETOUQUE & to move again if required. This move was well & secretly done. ZC	

WAR DIARY
INTELLIGENCE SUMMARY
(Erase heading not required.)

Army Form C. 2.

Instructions regarding War Diaries and Intelligence Summaries are contained in F.S. Regs. Part II. and the Staff Manual respectively. Title pages will be prepared in manuscript.

Place	Date	Hour	Summary of Events and Information	Remarks and references to Appendices
Near PROEGSTEERT	24.11.15		The enemy's artillery was more active to-day – Aged many shells fell in various parts of the line & my Batteries fired in Retaliation &c	
	25.11.15	10 a.m.	"A" Battle Practice was carried out this morning by the B.G.C.R.A. from 10 to 12.30	
		10.45 a.m.	ST YVES & THE CONVENT were shelled during the morning. A small working party at U 21.6.6½.3 was stopped working by a few shells from "D" Battery &c	
	26.11.15	10 a.m.	The enemy's Artillery left us alone to-day – "A" Battery harassed the New M.G. emplacement at U.28.a.4.i.8 & "D" Battery again dealt with a working party at U.21.6.7.3½.	
		9.10 p.m.	2nd Lieut TOMAR attached R.A.E. whilst another German Periscope from Trench 120 &c	
	27.11.15	1.30 a.m.		
		3.10 p.m.	Two guns of "D" Battery one near ESSEX FARM & one close to the Battery portion co-operated with the 29th Division by enfilading the Trenches S of the River LYS at E. 17. a. 6. 3. – 100 rounds were fired from one gun & 26 from the other – half the rounds between 3 x 3.10 pm & the other half between 3.25 x 3.35 pm. The Result was satisfactory and the B.G.C.R.A 21st Division sent his thanks to the Battery for its useful work. – Hazel post – 2c	
	28.11.15		Except for the usual shelling of PROEGSTEERT & the German Artillery opposite. German Aeroplanes were active and circled over Battery positions &c a good deal during the day. Our Aeroplane Guns appeared to be having them severely alone. – A very hard frost all day – but the weather seems likely to break. 2c	
	29.11.15		A very misty wet day. Very little observation possible. – PROEGSTEERT was shelled as usual &c	
	30.11.15		Enemy's Artillery more active. ST YVES & AUBREER were both shelled – Nothing else to report 2c	

III ᵗᵉ Bde: R.2.a.
Vol: 4

12/7809

25ᵗʰ Kumaun

Kac 15

Vol. III

Army Form C. 2118.

WAR DIARY
or
INTELLIGENCE SUMMARY
(Erase heading not required.)

Instructions regarding War Diaries and Intelligence Summaries are contained in F. S. Regs., Part II. and the Staff Manual respectively. Title pages will be prepared in manuscript.

Place	Date	Hour	Summary of Events and Information	Remarks and references to Appendices
In Gun Positions 9? PL&E.G. STEERT	1.12.15		A minor operation was carried out with a view to bombarding FACTORY FARM. Batteries of my Brigade took part and did useful work in bombarding Trenches (numerating) Trenches in that neighbourhood. 2C	
	2.12.15	10 a.m.	Batteries occupied with "Battle Practice" from 10 a.m to 12.30pm - LtCOETE carried the Scheme out in the Bn" Artillery - Major McLelland, "A" Battery (commanded the Brigade) The Germans exploded a trench Mine opposite Trench 99 and my "D" Battery retaliated on Trenches opp. 102 -	
		6.30pm	A generally quiet day. 2C	
	3.12.15		An abnormally quiet day on our front. Very wet and misty.	
		9.45am	A German Sniper in Trench 120 was seen playing Hockey too & the Sniper Aimes on the Trench - The worlds at V.28.a.5.7. & V.28.a.4.6 are becoming too strong for any serious damage to the done by 18Pdr Am G 2C	
	4.12.15		A very wet misty day. The enemy's Artillery was not active 2C	
	5.12.15	11.30 am	"A" Battery opened a working party very S about V.24.C.9.0 and (carrying completed iron. This party was engaged in something in the nature of a Sap & is reported to be in (course of) construction under the wire in the wire down. Our trenches know the Story work at V.28.a.5.7 V.24.d.0.2½ DEVIEMONT appears to be a standard spot with the Germans in that neighbourhood, was shelled during the day by "B" Battery. This caused rapid retaliation by the Germans. 2C	
	6.12.15		A stormy day. Much traffic was seen by LIEUT HIGGS "D" Battery on the WARNETON Road at V.12.a - "A" Battery also knocked a machine gun emplacement about locally at V.28.b.6.2½.90	
	7.12.15		Army Quiet Day - All my Batteries now put 2 shells daily into the BIRDCAGE 2C	

Army Form C. 2118.

WAR DIARY
or
INTELLIGENCE SUMMARY.
(Erase heading not required.)

Vol III

Instructions regarding War Diaries and Intelligence Summaries are contained in F. S. Regs., Part II. and the Staff Manual respectively. Title pages will be prepared in manuscript.

Place	Date	Hour	Summary of Events and Information	Remarks and references to Appendices
In Gun Positions PLOEGSTEERT	8.12.15		Nothing of interest to Report. ge	
	9.12.15		The enemy's Artillery was much more active. PLOEGSTEERT - MESSINES - PLOEGSTEERT Road was shelled during the day. LE GHEER also received attention. A few day not much more. 2 of my Batteries were held in readiness for a special purpose to-night, but the enterprise was abandoned. ge	
	10.12.15	5.15 p.m.	"C" Battery's Gun Position & Billets came in for 8 or 9 Shells - 2 of which fell in the farm house & barn where the officers & men billeted there were no casualties. ge	
	11.12.15		A quiet day. The enemy's desultory shelling on both sides. "C" Battery began changing its position & moved one section to-night. ge	
	12.12.15		Another very quiet day. Nothing to report. ge	
	13.12.15		The enemy's Artillery was more active to-day. One Section of "B" Battery was pushed forward to a position near MOUNTAIN GUN FARM to engage a suspected O.P. I was myself present in the O.P. and after an hour's firing - the enemy turned whizz-bangs onto one of the guns - there were no casualties. The O.P. was also shelled in the afternoon. The section was safely withdrawn in the evening. LIEUT. HIGGS. "D" Battery made a Reconnaissance of the BIRDCAGE and gave some useful information. ge	
	14.12.15		A very quiet day. Nothing to report. ge	
	15.12.15		No hostile fire in my zone to-day - "D" Battery began making new emplacements at U.19.d.6.2.M.2. for a section which is to be handed over tactically to the R.I. Division with a view to replacing Trenches in C.17.1.A. ge	
	16.12.15		Nothing to report - except a certain amount of hostile fire on AUCHER, CORRENT, & LANCASHIRE SUPPORT FARM, provoked by "A" Battery ranging Trenches & about at V.28.a.6.4. ge	

WAR DIARY
INTELLIGENCE SUMMARY
(Erase heading not required.)

Army Form C. 2118.

Vol III

Instructions regarding War Diaries and Intelligence Summaries are contained in F. S. Regs., Part II. and the Staff Manual respectively. Title pages will be prepared in manuscript.

Place	Date	Hour	Summary of Events and Information	Remarks and references to Appendices
In Front Positions near PLOEGSTEERT	17.12.15	10 a.m.	A quiet day — Foggy and wet. Not much doing — "Battle Practice" occupied my Batteries in the morning —	
		12 noon	Transport was heard on the HALTE–PONT–ROUGE ROAD, also a platoon of it, relieved 8 Staffs. I.C.	
	18.12.15	7.30 p.m.	A very quiet day — Nothing of interest I.C.	
	19.12.15	4.20 a.m.	Enemy's batteries more active. Two shells fell near "D" Battery position but were evidently stray shots. I.C.	
	20.12.15	2.6 3 p.m.	A small operation with the object of destroying a work at V.28.a.4½.6 by Col. Cooke was commenced. "A" Battery & Trench Mortars D/113, & Trench "A" Battery took part. A good deal of retaliation but no casualties —	
			Successful bombardment —	
			During bombardment an experiment was carried out by "B" & "B" Battery which had been moved forward. To test fire fired with settings for Ranges up to 4500 yds — Bursts occurred at the muzzle except at settings at 8 & 1. Where a fair percentage of bursts were observed by flank observers — The gun was not treated at first but when the experiment was over a few rounds of the enemy being I close to a position. No casualties — It is not apparent to Troops that have to do with — become up set at very short settings —	
	22.12.15		A false alarm of a fair attack at 7 p.m.	
	23.12.15		Very wet & foggy. Nothing to report. I.C. Working parties — Sniper's Tree I.C. engaged but nothing special occurred. I.C.	

Army Form C. 2118.

WAR DIARY
or
INTELLIGENCE SUMMARY.

(Erase heading not required.)

Instructions regarding War Diaries and Intelligence Summaries are contained in F. S. Regs., Part II. and the Staff Manual respectively. Title pages will be prepared in manuscript.

Place	Date	Hour	Summary of Events and Information	Remarks and references to Appendices
In gun position	23-12-15		Nothing of importance.	
	24-12-15		Working parties dispersed, but nothing of importance. Colonel Clarke assumed command of 25th Divl. Artillery during absence on leave of Brig Gen Bethell. Command of Bde devolved upon Major MacLellan. "A" Batty. gun answer further gunner.	
PLOEGSTEERT	25-12-15			
	26-12-15		Working parties fired on & dispersed.	
	27-12-15		Ditto	
	28-12-15		Working parties dispersed and casualties caused. Traffic was shelled on road S. of PETITE HAIE farm and a gun, where plant was spotted by the infantry, was engaged at U28.L.89½. "B" Batty took part in a minor operation. "C" Batty fired 72 rounds on infantry in front of the enemy S.O.S. call from infantry in front of them. The enemy fired in retaliation on AU GHEER and S.E. corner of PLOEGSTEERT.	
	29-12-15		Nothing.	
	30-12-15		Nothing of importance; a few rounds at various targets. Bt. F. Gutteridge, "C" Batty, wounded whilst at the O.P.	
	31-12-15		Nil.	

31/12/15

G.P.MacLellan
Major R.A.
Comdg. 111th Bde. R.F.A.

25th. DIVISION
ARTILLERY

111th. BRIGADE R. F. A.

25th. DIVISIONAL ARTILLERY

JANUARY 1916.

WAR DIARY
INTELLIGENCE SUMMARY

Army Form C. 2118.

Vol. 5.

Instructions regarding War Diaries and Intelligence Summaries are contained in F.S. Regs., Part II. and the Staff Manual respectively. Title pages will be prepared in manuscript.

(Erase heading not required.)

Place	Date	Hour	Summary of Events and Information	Remarks and references to Appendices
In position near PLOEGSTEERT	1-1-16	0.0 a.m.	A dozen rounds were put into the Birdcage and about 20 into DEULEMONT as New Year greetings from the enemy.	
	2-1-16		A few rounds at working parties & buildings. Enemy shelled on O.P. at LONDON Farm, and AU GHEER.	
	3-1-16		Enemy shelled and damaged very much "B" Battery O.P at LONDON Farm.	
	4-1-16		Nothing.	
	5-1-16		Enemy again shelled LONDON Farm. Batteries fired a few rounds at parties of enemy.	
	6-1-16		"C" Battery shelled DEULEMONT Church. Small results.	
	7-1-16		The usual few rounds at various targets.	
	8-1-16		Our O. Pot- LONDON FARM was again shelled - We put some rounds into The BIRDCAGE. A quiet day otherwise. SC	
	9-1-16	3.45 p.m.	LONDON FARM & MOUNTHIN GUN FARM were shelled - These places appear to be generally shelled when our own Artillery shell. HL- ECLUSES CHIMNEY.- "A" Battery dispersed a Working Party at PONT ROUGE in the morning. Several direct hits were obtained by the same Battery on DEULEMONT CHURCH. R.S.M. S.E. HAYES has left the Brigade on promotion to 2. LIEUT. SC	
	10.1.16		Enemy's Artillery was much more active to-day. PLOEGSTEERT was shelled and 2 guns "D" Battery which were registering from a forward position at CALVAIRE FARM were located & shelled. No guns were withdrawn at night & there were no casualties. A suspected Gas cylinder was seen in the enemy's trenches & engaged by B Battery; a few hits were made in it- but no gas came out- It was only 4' by 8" or so the gun firing at it had to be ouchoned. SC	
	11.1.16		The 2 guns of "D" Battery withdrawn last night to a position further back. took part in a saddle of operation (arried out by 21st Divs Inft. The D guns enfiladed the enemy trenches near D.17 and although communication was interrupted for 3/4 hour the firing continued correctly. SC	

WAR DIARY
or
INTELLIGENCE SUMMARY
(Erase heading not required.)

Army Form C. 2118.

Place	Date	Hour	Summary of Events and Information	Remarks and references to Appendices
In positions Batteries	12.1.16 to 13.1.16	3.20 p.m.	A quiet day. The wood behind Trench 118 & PLOEGSTEERT were shelled - DOUVE MINT was shelled in retaliation.	
PLOEGSTEERT		9.p.m	The PIGGERIES were shelled & the Infantry billetted there scattered round the Mid Theatre. The PIGGERIES in PLOEGSTEERT WOOD 2C. C. Battery silenced a hostile Trench MORTAR 2C	
			D. Battery in PLOEGSTEERT WOOD 2C	
	13.1.16 14.1.16	4.15 p.m	C Battery was firing H.E. Shell fuse 100 - when at the 124 round burst in the bore & blew the muzzle from the gun & damaged the wheels. The breech block held and no one was injured. A quiet day 2C	
	14.1.16		CALVAIRE FARM was heavily shelled - the actual position where "D" Battery had had 2 guns in the 10th being hit. several times - GUNNER'S FARM was also shelled as soon as the enemy guns had finished with CALVAIRE FARM - KEEPER'S HUT received a few shells. This is where "D" Battery is consolidating a position for 2 guns 2C	
	15.1.16		Nothing to note - to-day. 2C	
	16.1.16		Nothing to report 2C	
	17.1.16		2 guns of D Battery moved to KEEPER'S HUT. One other Royals moved to LOOPHOLE FARM was shelled by "A" Battery during the afternoon & several direct hits were obtained. 2C	
	18.1.16		A very quiet day - No hostile fire reported in this Zone. Batteries occupied in the Registration	
	19.1.16	12.30 to 5.25 p.m.	A minor operation against the LE TOUQUET SALIENT was successfully carried out to-day by 9th & 11th Infs & the 26th Div 7 Art. All the Batteries of this Brigade took part & performed the tasks of Wire-cutting, bombarding & barraging in a satisfactory manner. A Battery cut 2 guns forward at U.2.8.d.1.2.½. cut 2 lanes of wire each 10 yards wide with 227 rounds of Shrapnel. 2 guns of D Battery which bombarded BROWN KEEPER'S HUT a very forward position were heavily shelled. 2nd LIEUT. MILLER was in charge & did very well. He succeeded in silencing the fire until his R was completed. This role & men wounded & many others bruised by pieces of Shrapnel. Gas was used by us during the operation. The trenches at LE TOUQUET were very much battered by guns & Trench MORTARS 2C	

Army Form C. 2118.

WAR DIARY
or
INTELLIGENCE SUMMARY.
(Erase heading not required.)

Instructions regarding War Diaries and Intelligence Summaries are contained in F. S. Regs., Part II. and the Staff Manual respectively. Title pages will be prepared in manuscript.

Place	Date	Hour	Summary of Events and Information	Remarks and references to Appendices
Guns in action near PROECSTEERT	20.1.16		Notwithstanding yesterday's operation there was very little hostile fire to-day. In fact it was an unusually quiet day. SC	
	21.1.16	8.10 a.m	Working Party at V.28.6.6.6. dispersed by A Battery, & later a French Tramway at V.28.6.5.6 was damaged by the same Battery. SC	
	22.1.16		Nothing to note. SC	
	23.1.16		LOOPHOLE FARM was once more shelled by A Battery - The ruins appear to have been strengthened for use as an O.P. and 18 p.2 H.E. have now not much effect against A quiet day. Very foggy early. SC	
	24.1.16		A quiet day except for the shelling of AV. GHEER. A Battery's O.P. About 35 H.E. shell were put in & round it and the telephonists who were in a cellar which was also well sandbagged suffered - One was severely wounded in the head, & another in the buttock, a 3rd man was suffering from shock. The shell which set the damage came into the cellar. SC	
	25.1.16	9.55 p.m.	A quiet day - Hardly any hostile fire reported - 2 guns of D Battery which are tactically attached to 21st Div: Artillery took part in a Minor operation at 2.15. Div:n The Trenches about C.17 Central were bombarded these guns at 9.55 p.m. There is a keen war at a point opposite Trench 104 - This is evidently of some importance as the damage done to it by B Battery a day or two ago was attempted to be repaired - On each occasion guns of B Battery stopped the work. SC	
	26.1.16		A very quiet day. Nothing to report. SC	
	27.1.16		A quiet day. Except that AV.GHEER. O.P had 50 shells put in & round it. There were 2 direct hits & one telephonist was slightly wounded. SC	

WAR DIARY
or
INTELLIGENCE SUMMARY.
(Erase heading not required.)

Army Form C. 2118.

Place	Date	Hour	Summary of Events and Information	Remarks and references to Appendices
Guns in Position near PLOEGSTEERT	28.11.16		Batteries begin to move out of positions to go into Reserve — being relieved by guns of the 9th Divisional Artillery. — The Head Quarters of the relieving Brigade arrives to take over to-day — 1 Section of each Battery marches to CAESTRE. Lieut-Col- E.S. BROOKE relieves me — and during the afternoon visits gun positions with me. A good deal of shelling between PLOEGSTEERT & LE BIZET ROAD.	
	29.11.16		B & H Quadrants & remaining Sections of Batteries march to CAESTRE (12 Miles) — units arrive intown respective billets during the afternoon at 9.15 a.m. Billets fair only.	
	30.11.16		Batteries occupied in cleaning up, and overhauling their equipment. Very foggy day.	
	31.11.16		Batteries engaged in general overhauling & necessary repairs. Foggy day. 2 October. EC	

E Clarke
Col. R.A.
O.C. 111th Bde R.F.A

25th. DIVISION

ARTILLERY

111th. BRIGADE R. F. A.

25th. DIVISIONAL ARTILLERY

F E B R U A R Y 1 9 1 6.

WAR DIARY
or
INTELLIGENCE SUMMARY

Army Form C. 2118.

Place	Date	Hour	Summary of Events and Information	Remarks and references to Appendices
CAESTRE	1.2.16		Brigade in rest at CAESTRE. The usual drills etc. EC	
	2.2.16		Ditto. Ditto. EC	
	3.2.16		Ditto Ditto EC	
BOLLEZEELE	4.2.16		The Brigade marches to the Oudezeele Training Area near WATTEN 18½ miles - Start at 8.30.a.m. via ST SYLVESTRE - ZUYDPEENE (midday Halt) - NOORDPEENE - LE MENEGAT - RUBROUCK - BOLLEZEELE where the Brigade Billets - Arrive at BOLLEZEELE at 4.p.m. - Some rain during the march. EC	
	5.2.16		Batteries settle down into their Billets which are good - The training is composed of various small fields into which Batteries marys? (came into action but a) great deal of work has to be done on the Roads - and Stables work can be very usefully done. EC	
	6.2.16		Batteries training - Drill Order - Skeleton Battery Staffs. etc.	
	7.2.16		Lieut & Adjt CONDERTON pros to a course of lectures at BAILLEUL. LIEUT. CAMPION "D" Battery is to perform the duties. - A Battery out in marching Order - Rode with the 13 R.C.R? to fire it at work - Other Batteries continuing training. Hail & rain. EC	
	8.2.16		Brigade Scheme in Skeleton. - Practice in Communications & taking up positions quickly - Frost at night. EC	
	9.2.16		Some reconnoitring & Batteries continuing their training. - Frost at night. EC	
	10.2.16		Reconnaissance and Battery Training. EC	
	11.2.16		Very wet day. Brigade Scheme & Inspection by Gen'l Sir H. PLUMER (4nd Army) cancelled. EC	
	12.2.16		Brigade Scheme. Gen. Sir H. PLUMER & Gen. DORAN arrive and see the working of the Scheme. - Orders received that Batteries are to be prepared to move at 24 hours notice EC	
	13.2.16		Getting ready to march. Back to CAESTRE to-morrow. - Church Parade at 4.p.m. EC	

Army Form C. 2118.

WAR DIARY
or
INTELLIGENCE SUMMARY.
(Erase heading not required.)

Place	Date	Hour	Summary of Events and Information	Remarks and references to Appendices
BOLLEZEELE to CAESTRE	14.2.16		Windy & rainy early, but clears later - Marched - 8. a.m. for CAESTRE - Halt at ZUYT PEENE from 10.30 to 11.56 a.m. Genl. DORAN sees the Brigade go by & expresses himself pleased with its appearance. Arrive CAESTRE at 3.15 p.m. into Billets - Shortly after arrival the Hd. Qrs. Barn) & the Pioneer Battalion (S.W. B) is on fire and very pr. work is done by "D" Battery in putting it out - 2C	
CAESTRE	15.2.16		Training in the morning - Football Tournament in afternoon 2C	
"	16.2.16		Very windy day. The usual Training & Football 9C	
"	17.2.16		LIEUT & ADJT. A. ANDERTON leaves for the Infantry (ordered) A. Battery No 4 of 13 me. At 8. a.m. an order is received for a Test, Turn out as if for a move - The Brigade is formed up at the Rendez-vous by 10.30 a.m. - Inspection by B.G.C.R.A. 2C	
"	18.2.16		The usual Training & football in the afternoon 2C	
"	19.2.16		A Divisional Training Scheme is circulated - Conference with my Battery Commanders about it, in the evening 2C	
"	20.2.16		Cold & frosty. Church Parade at 5.30. p.m. 2C	
"	21.2.16		A Battery goes to STEENVOORDE as instructional Battery at 2nd Army School. Outdoor Scheme for F.O.C.R.A - in the neighborhood of MONT DES CATS - Out from 8am till 12.30 p.m. 2C	
"	22.2.16		Snowing - Nothing to record 2C	
"	23.2.16		Cold, frosty & snow - Nothing to record 2C	
"	24.2.16		Cold, frost & snow on the ground - Give a lecture to officers of the Brigade on ESPRIT DE CORPS and Discipline - In the evening receive a wire cancelling all leave -	

WAR DIARY
or
INTELLIGENCE SUMMARY.
(Erase heading not required.)

Army Form C. 2118.

Place	Date	Hour	Summary of Events and Information	Remarks and references to Appendices
CAESTRE	25.2.16		Snow & frost - slight thaw in afternoon & evening - but freezes again at night - Divisional "Scheme with Battery Commanders" - owing to the weather a Scheme for G.O.C.R.A. is cancelled.	
"	26.2.16		Go with 13 G.C.R.A. to MONT DE MERRIS. Meet G.O.C. Division Staff etc and we all poured over the ground over which the Divisional Scheme has been worked out - from 9 a.m. to 1 p.m. - At 7 p.m. receive orders that the Brigade is to be ready to move by Rail at 9 hours notice & that the Relief of 21st Division by us is cancelled until further orders. & LIEUT LIEUT CAMPION is now performing the duties of Adj'' in the absence of LIEUT ANDERTON - Snow in the morning - Thaw in afternoon. More snow at night.	
"	27.2.16		More snow. Thaw later - B.C's go to ARMENTIÈRES to look at the new positions there -. No Church Parade.	
	28.2.16		Motor at 9 a.m. with 13.G. BELL ell to ARMENTIÈRES - Look at some positions with Gen'. WELLESLEY & Col. BANISTER. At 2. return owing to orders -. Orders are to be ready to move by road & rail at 48 hours notice.	
	29.2.16		Nothing to record.	

E. Clarke Col R.A.
C"" 111 L. 13" P.F.A.

<u>25th. DIVISION</u>

<u>ARTILLERY</u>

<u>111th. BRIGADE R. F. A.</u>

<u>25th. DIVISIONAL ARTILLERY</u>

<u>M A R C H 1 9 1 6.</u>

Army Form C. 2118.

WAR DIARY
or
INTELLIGENCE SUMMARY.
(Erase heading not required.)

Instructions regarding War Diaries and Intelligence Summaries are contained in F. S. Regs., Part II. and the Staff Manual respectively. Title pages will be prepared in manuscript.

Place	Date	Hour	Summary of Events and Information	Remarks and references to Appendices
CAESTRE	1.3.16		Brigade still at rest – Awaiting orders to move. 2C	
"	2.3.16		Take B.C's & officers out over ground in connection with a Divisional Scheme 2C	
"	3.3.16	9 a.m	Divisional Artillery Scheme – 2C	
"	4.3.16		Snowing and very cold – The usual Training going on 2C	
"	5.3.16		Church Parade. 2C 2nd LIEUT CHIDWELL succeeds 2nd LT. EVANS as Orderly Officer	
"	6.3.16		Some snow. 2C	
"	7.3.16		Still bad weather with snow. 2C Div. Art. Scheme has to be abandoned in/consequence	
"	"		Frost & snow all day – Heavy fall of snow at night 2C	
"	8.3.16		of the weather. Nothing to record. 2C	
"	"		Snow lying thick –	
"	9.3.16		LIEUT PARKINS from Adjt: 112 & 13 all succeeds Capt. DUDLEY in command of the B.A.C	
"	"		The latter is attached to Div'n' Head Quarters – 2nd LIEUT CHIDWELL goes off as billeting officer to MAZINGHEM. Orders to move South received 2C	
MAZIN-GHEM –	10.3.16		March at 9.30.a.m – About 18 miles – go by AIRE to MAZINGHEM & FONTES. Arrive 2.p.m – good billets – 2C	
BOYAVAL	11.3.16		March at 9. About 12 miles – good march – cold much snow lying about – Reach BOYAVAL at 1.30 – Steep hill up to BOYAVAL from HEDCHIN – 2 Batteries billetted at EPS –	
"	12.3.16		Thawing but fine sunny day. 2C	
"	13.3.16		Fine weather – Gun Drill Signaling & c 2C	
"	14.3.16		Fine weather – much warmer. The usual Training. 2C	

Army Form C. 2118.

WAR DIARY
or
INTELLIGENCE SUMMARY.
(Erase heading not required.)

Instructions regarding War Diaries and Intelligence Summaries are contained in F. S. Regs., Part II. and the Staff Manual respectively. Title pages will be prepared in manuscript.

Place	Date	Hour	Summary of Events and Information	Remarks and references to Appendices
BOYAVAL	15.3.16	—	The usual training – nothing of importance to record. 2℅	
"	16.3.16	—	Orders to move tomorrow received at 9.30 p.m. Same Operation Orders for 17th March. 2℅	
ORLINCOURT	17.3.16	—	March at 9 a.m. via EPS – HESTRUS – ORIAS to ORLINCOURT. – Fair billets but great scarcity of water. 2℅	
"	18.3.16	—	Settling Brigade in. – Nothing to record. 2℅	
"	19.3.16	—	Motor to MAROEIL to reconnoitre positions in G.H.Q. 2 Line. Country very bare and open. – Fine day. – Go to Mt. ST. ELOY and get a good view. – Write report. 2℅	
"	20.3.16	—	The usual training. Brigade still in Reserve having joined the 17th Corps. of the 3rd Army. 2℅	
"	21.3.16	—	Damp drizzly weather. – Nothing to record. 2℅	
"	22.3.16	—	Still damp foggy weather. Nothing to record. The usual training 2℅	
"	23.3.16	—	Nothing to record. 2℅	
"	24.3.16	—	Colonel Hoste assumed command of 25 Div. Arty, during absence on leave of Brig. Gen. Bettam. Major G.P. MacClellan assumed command of 111th Brigade R.F.A. pro. tem. Qu	
"	25.3.16 to 30.3.16	—	Nothing to record. Qu	
"	31-3-16	—	The Commander in Chief, Sir Douglas Haig, inspected batteries of the brigade at their ordinary parades Qu	

G.P. MacClellan Major R.A.
Comdg. 111th Bde. R.F.A.

25th. DIVISION

ARTILLERY

111th. BRIGADE R. F. A.

25th. DIVISIONAL ARTILLERY

APRIL 1916.

WAR DIARY
or
INTELLIGENCE SUMMARY
(Erase heading not required.)

Army Form C. 2118.

Instructions regarding War Diaries and Intelligence Summaries are contained in F. S. Regs., Part II. and the Staff Manual respectively. Title pages will be prepared in manuscript.

Place	Date	Hour	Summary of Events and Information	Remarks and references to Appendices
ORLENCOURT and MONCHY BRETON (In rest billets)	1st April		Hd. Qrs.	
	2"		Colonel Choate proceeded on leave home. 3 Officers & 90 men attached to Hd.Qr. 4th Div. R.A. for digging in trenches on the front line.	
	3"		Hd. Qr.	
	8"			
	9"		Colonel Choate returns from leave & assumes command of Brigade. Colonel Clock proceeded to Infantry school. Command upon direction on Major G.P. MacLennan	
	10"			
	11" to 13"		Hd. Qrs.	
	14"		Col. Clock returns from the Infantry Senior Officer's Course. Very cold day with hail. The Corps Commander Lt. Gen. BYNG inspected the Brigade on a route march. Bring before him the question of forage which has been very short for the past fortnight. 2C	
	15"		Still cold – some snow – 2C	
	16"		Motor to our new front to see new positions etc we are going to take up in front of NEUVILLE-ST VAAST etc. Finer day 2C Bad weather 2C	
	17"		Very wet day, B.C.'s up to the line to inspect positions 2C	
	18"		Still cold & disagreeable weather 2C	
	19"		Finer in the morning but very wet later – B.C.'s & signallers go up to the line to learn the front 2C	
x 20"			Bad weather 2C	

Army Form C. 2118.

WAR DIARY
or
INTELLIGENCE SUMMARY.
(Erase heading not required.)

Instructions regarding War Diaries and Intelligence Summaries are contained in F.S. Regs., Part II. and the Staff Manual respectively. Title pages will be prepared in manuscript.

Place	Date	Hour	Summary of Events and Information	Remarks and references to Appendices
ORLENCOURT (in and about)	April 22nd		nil.	
	23rd		Colonel Cloete went to senior officers conference at St Pol. Major MacClellan arranged command.	
Guns in position in Gun Pits W9-S-W-B NEUVILLE St VAAST			One section of each battery went up into line in relief of 1st Hyde Midland Bde. R.F.A. W. and S.W. of NEUVILLE St VAAST; wagon line and B.A.G. at ACQ. The whip was carried out without any hitch. "A" Battery has one gun in a detached position to enfilade trenches further S. Qu.	
NEUVILLE St VAAST	24th		Section in the line registered. A Batty was heavily shelled. One direct hit was received on a gun pit, damaging it and a gun wheel; Gun out of action until evening on account of the collapse of the gun pit. No casualties. Qu.	
"	25th		Remaining sections came up into the line, and completed relief of 1st N.M. Bde. R.F.A. Gun	
"	26th		"A" "C" and "D" Batty's shelled. Another direct hit on a gun pit of A Batty, another gun wheel damaged. Gun temporarily out of action. Qu.	
"	27th		A.B. and C. Batty fired 94, 13, and 24 rounds respectively in retaliation for heavy bombardment of our trenches by the enemy. Qu.	
"	28th	10.15am 11am	Batteries occupied with Registration. All Batteries fired in retaliation called for by Infantry & C Battery received an S.O.S call & fired 96 rounds between 10 p.m. & 12 midnight. Col Cloete returns from Senior Artillery Officers Course & resumes Command.	
"	29th		Batteries registering. "D" Battery fired 50 rx at front line of craters 6 & 7 at request of Infantry - 2C	
"	30th		Registration. A retaliaire account of guns firing by the Batteries a quiet day. Registration at the call of the Infantry	

E Cloete
Col R A
C W/111 W/3 W. R.F.A

25th. DIVISION

ARTILLERY

111th. BRIGADE R. F. A.

25th. DIVISIONAL ARTILLERY

MAY 1916.

Army Form C. 2118.

111 Bde R.F.A.
XX Vol 8 A

WAR DIARY
or
INTELLIGENCE SUMMARY.
(Erase heading not required.)

Instructions regarding War Diaries and Intelligence Summaries are contained in F. S. Regs., Part II. and the Staff Manual respectively. Title pages will be prepared in manuscript.

Place	Date	Hour	Summary of Events and Information	Remarks and references to Appendices
In gun Positions W of NEUVILLE ST VAAST.	1.5.16	—	Nothing special to record — Batteries busy registering	&c
"	2.5.16	"	" " " " "	&c
"	3.5.16	"	" " " " "	&c
"	4.5.16	"	D Battery did some damage to the enemy's Support Trenches at A.4.b.2.2. at the request of the Infantry — A Battery's Emplacement fired at A.14.a.3½.1. was Knocked about by the enemy, did the afternoon & a deal registered damage.	&c
"	5.5.16	4.p.m	Enemy's Artillery active. About 52 p^d 4.2 H fell in the neighborhood of D B Battery's position at 5.30 p.m. No damage.	&c
"	6.5.16	3.40 p.m 5.30 pm	D Battery's Position at A7.01.4.3 was heavily shelled — About 85 rounds were fired at it. One gun was damaged — 1 a.D to the entrance at night. Enemy's Artillery inactive. Our Batteries continued registering & strafing Working Parties etc.	&c
"	7.5.16.		No hostile fire — Registration & shelling of Working Party at A.4 by our Batteries	&c
"	8.5.16		A very quiet day. — A small shoot in the evening by 51st ON at. My Batteries strafing	&c
"	9.5.16		The shelling S.23.C.3.3. & S.23.d.45.38. by D Battery brought retaliation on AV.R.12.72	
"	10.5.16		Dieming Station — retaliated on S.30.a.5.2 (Dump) write A & B Batteries at 8 p.m	&c
"	11.5.16	12.30 p.m	B Batty dispersed a working party at A5.6.3.5 & at 5.30 p.m. had a very successful shoot at a Trench Tramway at A.4 (ruled in conjunction with the Infantry. C & D Batteries shelled the Dump at S.30.a.6.2 and brought retaliation on	&c
"	12.5.16	5 p.m	The NEUVILLE AQ RIEZ Road. Our transport & wagon body write one of Blown up. One very Two Battery was Knocked out — & Battery's Position &c C Batty shelled enemy's Trenches in (I junction with infantry at 4.p at. Observers fairly quickly with little	&c

Army Form C. 2118.

WAR DIARY
or
INTELLIGENCE SUMMARY.
(Erase heading not required.)

Instructions regarding War Diaries and Intelligence Summaries are contained in F.S. Regs., Part II. and the Staff Manual respectively. Title pages will be prepared in manuscript.

Place	Date	Hour	Summary of Events and Information	Remarks and references to Appendices
In Gun Positions S.W. of NEUVILLE ST VAAST.	13.5.16	4.30 p.m.	"A" Battery did good shooting on enemy's trenches at A.4.d.5½.3.6 s at the request of Infantry.	
		5.50.	" " also by arrangement with Infantry shelled M.G. emplacements at A.5.a.b.4.8. "D" Battery did counter-Battery work at 8.p.m. Enemy Infantry active between 9 & 9.30.p.m. 2C.	
	14.5.16	4 p.m.	"C" Battery cooperated with Infantry & French Mortars & shelled the neighbourhood of Craters 8,6 & 1. Good results. Relief suspected between 8 & 10 p.m. All Batteries shelled the Communication Trenches. 2C	
	15.5.16	8.30 p.m.	D. Battery did minute-Battery work firing 9 & 2 rounds between 8.27 p.m. & 9.45 p.m. in conjunction with a Minor Operation in the Sector North of no. 2 C.	
	16.5.16	11 a.m.	A Shell fell on A Battery's Cupola & Gun Pit, doing some damage, but not to the Gun. A British aeroplane was seen to descend about F.30 in the evening — The occupants had been hit by aeroplane machine guns. 2C	
	17.5.16	9.30 a.m.	Gas Gongs heard — a false alarm. — Q Section are troubled out of a Crater 2C	
	18.5.16	3 a.m.	S.O.S. signal seen by a sentry — Written was evidently an error. —	
		2 p.m.	"C" Battery cooperated with Infantry & Trench Mortars & did some useful work at Trenches at A.4. 9. 6 - 2C.	
	19.5.16	1.20 p.m.	B & H² Q² shelled with 5.9. Shell. — Damage done slight. One Shell grazed C.O.'s dug out. & several were within 8 or 10 yds of H.Q. When & other pundits in the Trench.	
		2.30 p.m.	Much firing in our left at 8.30 p.m. — Assistance called for from my Batteries. — Firing ceased at 9.45 p.m. — No crater lost on 17th but retaken by their grenadiers 2C	
	20.5.16		Very quiet day on this front. Batteries occupied with Registration. with incoming Battery Officers. A B Battery did good Registration with Rite Balloon at A.11.a.9.9 & A.12.a.8.6 2C	
	21.5.16			

WAR DIARY
or
INTELLIGENCE SUMMARY

Army Form C. 2118.

Place	Date	Hour	Summary of Events and Information	Remarks and references to Appendices
Guns in action S.W. of NEUVILLE ST VAAST	21/5/16		Relief of Batteries intended to be night of Section B, C & D Batteries having been relieved on night of 19/20/5 – At 6 p.m. Enemy barrages & bombards Q sector & Trenches of Q sector & my batteries there as many guns as can reach target – the Dry Captures Q Trenches & 2 Platoons. Relief cancelled about 9 p.m. but as my batteries had been mostly Relief was carried out of B, C & D Batteries. A Battery & Head Quarters remained. A very busy night. Ammunition wrap as favorable during the night. Many lachrymatory shells used by the Germans causing a great deal of inconvenience & distress to the eyes &c	
Guns at ACQ except A Battery still in action	22/5/16		H.Q. & D still in the line. A very day – A Battery successfully got her guns out of them pits in daylight, in order to be able to turn her fire North on to P. & Q Sectors – Registration carried out – from 10.30 p.m. to 1.30 a.m. 30 rounds per hour were fired on to Trenches & own (captured) H.Q.rs received orders at 8 p.m. to move back to Wagon Lines during the night. This was done. "A" Battery was left in action. &c	
"	23/5/16		A Battery fired 592 Rounds during the night to support German Suffolk Trenches during an attack to the North. Remainder of Brigade in Wagon Lines &c	
"	24/5/16		A Battery under orders of O.C. 116th Brigade R.F.A. &c	
"	25/5/16		Halting to refit &c	
In action	26/5/16	4 p.m.	Busy day preparing to go back into action again – Relief completed by 11 p.m. Batteries in original positions. Quiet night &c	
"	27/5/16		Very quiet day. Batteries re-registering. B.A.C. abolished & becomes No. 4. Section B.D.A.C. &c	
"	28/5/16		Enemy's guns inactive. Working Parties observed & Retaliatory fire used & can't Infantry or Infantry observed to be preparing to move against us tonight. This dolled with materially. &c	
"	29/5/16		Very quiet day. Nothing to record except that Batteries began to be relieved – A Section of 13 Battery – C Battery to A.C.Q.	

WAR DIARY or INTELLIGENCE SUMMARY

Place	Date	Hour	Summary of Events and Information	Remarks and references to Appendices
Guns (less 2 Sections in action S.W. of NEUVILLE ST VAAST.)	30/5/16		A very quiet day. At 11.30 p.m. all my Batteries are relieved — and we go back to Wagon Lines at ACQ, arriving at about 12.45 a.m. 31.5.	
	31/5/16		Guns at ACQ, expecting to move to St MICHEL at night. At 6 p.m. received orders leaving Batteries less 2 Sections behind. H.Q. to move to ST MICHEL during the night. My Batteries remaining behind are A/111 a composite Batty 1/2 B/111 & 1/2 C/111 & my new Batty D C/113 (Howitzers) & becomes D/111 — 2ep. taxes my old D/111 — These Batteries all come under the orders of Lieut Col Baumbank DSO R.F.A.	

E Cloete
Col R.A.
Col. 111 & 13th Bde R.F.A.

25th. DIVISION

ARTILLERY

111th. BRIGADE R. F. A.

25th. DIVISIONAL ARTILLERY

J U N E   1 9 1 6.

A.A.G.
3rd Echelon. Base.

___

Herewith War Diary for the month of June 1916. of the 111th Brigade. R.F.A.

1-7-16

E. Cloete Col. R.A.
Comg 111th Bde R.F.A.

June

Army Form C. 2118.

111 R F A Vol 9

WAR DIARY
or
INTELLIGENCE SUMMARY.
(Erase heading not required.)

Place	Date	Hour	Summary of Events and Information	Remarks and references to Appendices
ROELLECOURT	1/6/16		Settling in Camp with H.Q. & "C" Battery in ST MICHEL WOOD by ROELLECOURT 2C	
1. Battery & H.Q.	2/6/16		Training Area about 5 miles from Camp. by MONCHY-LE-BRETON. — C. Battery Training Etc. GEN. DORAN handed over Division to Gen. BAINBRIDGE 2C	
3 Batteries in action under 51st Div. now	3/6/16		B.G.C.R.A. Ran a Skeleton Scheme for Div. Artillery ('Less 3 Batteries in the line) in Training Area. Weather cold 2C	
	4/6/16		Lecture by Lt. Col. BIRCH on "Training for the Offensive". Still cold 2C	
NEUVILLE ST. VAAST.	5/6/16		Training in Training Area for H.Q. & C. Battery. 2/3 Division W now in G.H.Q. Reserve 2C	
	6/6/16		R.A. Divisional Scheme for B.G.C.R.A. Very wet & cold 2C	
	7/6/16		Reconnoitring in Training Area — Showery and cold 2C	
	8/6/16		Artillery Scheme for B.G.C.R.A. in Training Area — Conference afterwards 2C	
	9/6/16		C. Battery & H.Q. 's out with 75th Inf. Brigade on a Scheme. Very showery & very chilly weather. 2C	
	10/6/16		Nothing to record. Heavy thunderstorm all the afternoon 2C	
	11/6/16		" " " . Still cold & wet. 2C	
	12/6/16		Divisional Scheme in Training Area. Very wet & cold 2C	
	13/6/16		Divisional " " Orders received to move to SCOCHES on OO TRE BOIS 6.2.15 b. 3 Batteries still in the line 2C	
	14/6/16		Getting ready to move — Nothing to record 2C	
	15/6/16		March at 10 a.m. to OO TRE BOIS (18 miles). Arrive at 4 p.m. 2C	

WAR DIARY

INTELLIGENCE SUMMARY

Army Form C. 2118.

Place	Date	Hour	Summary of Events and Information	Remarks and references to Appendices
OUTREBOIS	16/6/16		Rest at OUTREBOIS. Genl. BETHELL handed over command of 25th Divl. Artillery to Brig. Genl. KIRWAN. Finer weather.	
"	17/6/16		At 9 a.m. go with Genl. KIRWAN & the Staff Brigade Commanders to reconnoitre ground. NORTH of ALBERT. We go to a tea in the BOIS d'AVELUY, and see the various bridges over the ANCRE. Get back about 5 p.m. Move to FIEFFES by bright S.E.	
FIEFFES	18/6/16		At 8 a.m. go again to the front with other Officers of the Brigade to reconnoitre the same ground from a distance. We do not get in till 7 p.m. S.E. Raining (wm. of) A,B & D Batteries having come in. I go again with Batty. Commdrs. to reconnoitre the same ground. Got back at 8 p.m. ... S.E.	
"	19/6/16		Still cool but fine – Genl. KIRWAN inspects 'C' Battery at 11 a.m. – Lieut WEBB joins the Brigade – he has been in the H.A.C. – Col. CLOETE mentioned in Sir D. HAIG's Despatch which appeared in GAZETTE paper dated on 16/6/16 – S.E.	
"	20/6/16		Sent 10 of my Officers to the front reconnoitring – nothing else to record. go.	
"	21/6/16		Go reconnoitring – up to the front by Motor. Go to MARTINSART – & Trenches by PUISIEUX Post – AUTHUILLE wood. Every thing very quiet. Heavy Thunderstorms – S.E.	
"	22/6/16		Dawg, showery day – 1 Heavy Howitzer Battery + 1 bombardment on the front. Our Division in Army Reserve – attached x 6th Corps. S.E.	
"	23/6/16		Genl. KIRWAN inspects horses of A. B & D Batteries. Quite planned – 1st Day of Bombardment. S.E.	
"	24/6/16		Bombardment. S.E.	
"	25/6/16		Conference on Treatment with G.R.A. 2nd Day of Bombardment.	
"	26/6/16		3rd Day of Bombardment – Wet day – Officers to the front to reconnoitre. S.E.	

WAR DIARY
or
INTELLIGENCE SUMMARY.

Army Form C. 2118.

Place	Date	Hour	Summary of Events and Information	Remarks and references to Appendices
FIEFFES (In Reserve)	27/6/16		Very heavy rains on and off in the morning: In the afternoon Gen: KIRWAN inspects the Battery of this Brigade at Driving Drill &c — He seems quite satisfied that they are on an efficient as one might expect, considering that in many cases owing to Trench Warfare & difficulties of Training the men who acted as nos: 1 during Drill or otherwise has not been early practised. Orders received tomorrow a table part in Active Operations on 29th the Programme is (carried out) — The Division is in Mobile Reserve and moves as soon as the Evolution of the German Trenches (4th line) is effected — The Batteries will then move into positions about THIEPVAL. &c	
CONTAY (In reserve)	28/6/16		March at 9 am. Batteries at 50 minutes interval. Arrive CONTAY at intervals between 2.30 & 6 p.m. Final operations have been postponed and in consequence accommodation in CONTAY is not available — However by 8.30 p.m. a number of men & Batteries & billeting is agreed to by 4.9 th Division in whose area we are. Batteries get more or less settled in for the night — No further orders received during the night — The move to CONTAY was a very wet one — & the rain drenching &c.	
	29/6/16		Operation appears to be postponed — Nothing special to record. Weather is improving — at 11 p.m. Orders arrive notifying that Zero hour will now be at 1st June —.9c—	
	30/6/16		Fair weather — but still doubtful — H.Q. & 25th D.A. move in to CONTAY. Orders received that the expected Assault on German Trenches will take place 7.30 a.m. tomorrow. 25th Division is in army Reserve — but is expected to support the 32nd Division on 0 Thought it affect it has captured the "green line" — arriving from R.21 C. & E. & G.00 CU.S.E. FARM. 5.E.	
	30/6/16			E Crosbie Col R.A. Comg. III Bde R.F.A.

25th Div.

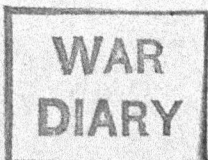

Headquarters,

111th BRIGADE, R.F.A.

J U L Y

1 9 1 6

WAR DIARY or INTELLIGENCE SUMMARY

Army Form C. 2118

111th Brigade R.F.A.

VOL / July

Place	Date	Hour	Summary of Events and Information	Remarks and references to Appendices
CONTAY	1/7/16		The Offensive of the British & French Commences — . Reconnoitring parties sent to SENLIS — but return at 4 p.m. as it does not appear as if tired would be any chance of the Batteries being able to advance across the River ANCRE to-day, as had been hoped. Our troops are held up at THIEPVAL. Fine warm day. — 2 C	
	2/7/16		Our troops are still held up in the neighbourhood of THIEPVAL & OVILLERS. A good many prisoners have been taken and I saw some at CONTAY who were unwounded — One Officer thought the Germans would soon take VERDUN and that they would three for more Terms of Peace — Batteries remain at CONTAY. SC	
	3/7/16		Preliminary orders received to relieve 32nd Divt Artillery in their Positions by the River ANCRE as they seem no chance of getting through at THIEPVAL to the movement — Batteries however are not moved to-night. But remain at CONTAY. 2C	
	4/7/16		Fresh orders not to take over gun positions of 32nd Divl Art. but to reconnoitre for new positions with centre line of zone on MOU-VET FARM — Go out in the afternoon with LIEUT. WEBB. very wet & a thunderstorm — We find positions in the open near MARTINSART and get back at 8 p.m. Batteries battle at CONTAY. 2C	
	5/7/16		3 & Battery Commanders go up reconnoitring round MARTINSART. Fix on certain positions in the open. At 11.12 get orders that Batteries are to move into positions to-night but nr near MARTINSART — Conference 7.30 Cap S & C R E's at 2. so & proceed to reconnoitre positions at W.15 — J. settle on 3 positions all in the open — C.12 battery is split up and A & B. Batteries become Gun Batteries for fire. Positions are at W.15.c & W.21.b. H Q at W.14.b. & H.3. Await arrival of Batteries.	
In action in the open S.E. of BOUZINCOURT	6/7/16		Batteries begin to come in at 1 a.m. get them settled in by 3. Work goes on most of the night — Batteries are to support OVILLERS. Batteries Report during the day in readiness for a barrage to commence — Positions much as on Salisbury Plain — Guns are hidden fr view of Fanzio hidden. 2C	

WAR DIARY or INTELLIGENCE SUMMARY

Army Form C. 2118.

Place	Date	Hour	Summary of Events and Information	Remarks and references to Appendices
Bn Station S.E. of BOUZAN-COURT	7/7/16		The Brigade took part in active operations in connection with an attack on OVILLERS by 12th Div. + 74th Inf. Brigade / 25th Division. The Brigade was employed in Barraging Trenches in X8 & X2 - The Howitzer Battery bombarded Strong Points in the same Area - The Batteries were shortly at a range of 4700 yds approx. - The Barrage was reported by an F.O.O. of 12" Dn." Artillery as Very good - No casualties - Capt. EDWARDES of 'C' Battery acted as LIAISON Officer with the left group / 124 D.A. and from time to time gave useful information as to the Progress of Operations - Observation of fire was almost impossible owing to the number of Shells in the air at the same time. - Hostile Artillery was inactive on our front and no shells fell anywhere near the Batteries of my Brigade. - The 2.6 gun 18 Pd. Batteries of the Brigade fired approximately 5500 Rounds The Howitzer Battery fired approximately 1530 " 20	
	8/7/16	2.45 pm	Batteries were almost continuously inactive on Barrage Lines N of OVILLERS. Weather was wet and unfavourable. - At 2.45 pm 'A' Battery reported a party of German Infantry at about X.2.c.9.5. advancing S.W. Fire was opened on them by A. Battery - Enemy were seen to retire. At 6 p.m. 'D' 13 Battery reported German soldiers were seen almost high running from X.2.d.0.3 - X.2.d.2.9. at 6 p.m. - The Day passed quietly and no hostile Shells fell near my Batteries - LIEUT. IRONSIDE / D Battery reconnoitred / W and B / from which to view the ground NE / OVILLERS. He went to MESNIL & reported the high ground as useless for the purpose. - He reported that from X.7.a.2.2. in trench Rubine on ONISTON STREET a view of about N2.b.99, X.2.c.2.7 - X.2.a.1.9. can be obtained. The German machine from strong point X2.99. at X.7.b.9.9. can be seen from Trench about X1.a. or 2. From line up to X.2.b.1c.9.3. can also be seen.	

WAR DIARY or INTELLIGENCE SUMMARY

Army Form C. 2118.

Place	Date	Hour	Summary of Events and Information	Remarks and references to Appendices
In action S.12.b BOUZINCOURT	9/7/16	3 p.m. 3.30 p.m.	The Batteries in action continuously day & night firing at irregular intervals on Barrage Lines N. OVILLERS – At 3 p.m. our Shell fire appears to have caused a large explosion in the village of POZIERES – At 3.30 p.m. the Germans opened a heavy fire behind OVILLERS & in region POZIERES – Batteries increased rate of fire. A small body of German prisoners was observed at the same time coming from the direction of LA BOISELLE in the direction of AVELUY – At 4 p.m. on the Germans opened a heavy fire on what appeared a numerous clerical coming from the direction of AUCHONVILLERS towards BEAUMONT HAMEL Capt. EDWARDS my Liaison Officer with Left Group 12 W.D. did a good deal of reconnoitring for use to-day, and at 12.5	
"	10/7/16		Batteries still in action in the open and on much the same Barrage Lines but with a rather reduced rate of fire – At 12.50 a.m. Captain EDWARDES sent me by despatch Rider a copy of Orders re operation intended to take place at 2 a.m. There might have proved invaluable as my Barrage Lines were somewhat where the attack on OVILLERS was intended – At 8 p.m. Captain EDWARDES was reported to have been wounded in the leg – No particulars – Wound not serious but would probably necessitate a trip to ENGLAND – Everything quiet round my Batteries – EC	
"	11/7/16		Batteries still in action on same Barrage Lines. LIEUT CALDWELL my Orderly Officer, & LIEUT WOODMAN A. BATTERY. made a reconnaissance for men into LA BOISELLE & x believe that to take and OVILLERS – chiefly with a view to finding an O.P. from which the ground N.E. of OVILLERS could be seen – The Reconnaissance was fraught with a good deal of danger as there.	

Army Form C. 2118.

WAR DIARY
or
INTELLIGENCE SUMMARY
(Erase heading not required.)

Place	Date	Hour	Summary of Events and Information	Remarks and references to Appendices
Trenches in the open N. of BOURAN COURT	12th July		These officers went in and out of trenches in close proximity to the enemy. The chief result of the Reconnaissance was that it was found that O.P's from which the country N.E of ONILLERS can be seen would have to be placed in X.14.a.b & c. but that O.P's further East would be useless. Orders received to take over positions now occupied by Batteries of 364 Bde. Artillery and to the Right Section of A.B. & D Batteries move into them in the afternoon and the whole of 'C' Battery in the evening. The positions are for forward at W.12.d.2.8 — W.12.d.2.2 — W.18.b.8.3 & W.18.d.2.8 respectively. Except in the case of 'C' Battery which moves into an unoccupied position, Batteries exchange guns with the Batteries they relieve. Wagon Lines do not move from their present position near BOURANCOURT. Firing on Barrage Lines continues all night with all available guns. E.G.	
In present positions W.18.b & W.18.d.	13th July		The remaining sections of A.B. & D Batteries move into the new positions during the afternoon. I go to my new Hd.Qrs & take over from Lieut. Col. SIMPSON but return to my old Hd.Qrs for the night — Batteries occupied in registering new Zones. E.G.	
	14th		At 7 a.m. move to my new H.Qrs. The Brigade is attached to the 12th Div. & Art. Group from which it takes its orders — Brigade belong to Reserve Artillery — and are covering 7th & 9th Inf. Bde. An attack by 26th Division was begun in accordance with Operation Orders attached	APPENDIX 1.

APPENDIX 1.

WAR DIARY
or
INTELLIGENCE SUMMARY
(Erase heading not required.)

Army Form C. 2118.

Place	Date	Hour	Summary of Events and Information	Remarks and references to Appendices
	14/7/16		and continued during the 14th. The Batteries under my command fired all day & night on Barrage Lines — There is nothing special to report except that it is believed the Barrages were effective as 12th Div. Artillery	Appendix 2
	15/7/16		The Batteries co-operated in the attack as detailed in 12th Divn. Artillery Operation Order No. 9 (attached) Appendix 2. At 5.30 p.m. Batteries took part in Bombardment of POZIERES. At 7.30 p.m. orders received to cut wire in front of POZIERES - Barrage about 3500x which is too long for effective wire cutting - It was too late to do much to-night 9C	
	16/7/16		Batteries were covering 143rd Brigade — 75th Bde having been called out of the line to-night — Barrage all day & night — Barrage by 13 army by X31.0Q — XO.678 reported on by O.C. Warwicks (14.3 & 13.A) at 5.30 p.m. 9C	
	17/7/16		Many forsshells fell round my H.Q. at 12.35 - 14.0 a.m. no casualties but few returned — wire - Batteries continue Barrages reported on POZIERES and then have returned in front of it - Difficult task Observation difficult - Barrage by heavy Eny. at 10.35 p.m. Barrage to help 143rd Bde — Own attack on POZIERES by the Infy on Right in which the Batteries were to have assisted does not seems to have Barraging & wire cutting continued — A gun etc day 9C	
	18/7/16			

WAR DIARY
INTELLIGENCE SUMMARY

Army Form C. 2118.

(Erase heading not required.)

Place	Date	Hour	Summary of Events and Information	Remarks and references to Appendices
Sausage Valley	19/7/16		A quiet day – Wire-cutting by A & B. 13. Batteries – A minor operation by 145th & 9th Brigades carried out to-night – Orders attached in accordance with the attached orders. S.C. The Brigade assisted in accordance with the attached orders. S.C. The 48th Infantry Division retired during the day.	Appendix 3
	20/7/16		Reports of infantry driven back retiring reportedly to reorganized during the day.S.C.	
	21/7/16		The 48th Division continued its attack early this morning in accordance with orders attached (Appendix 4). Once again the 111th Div. is ill prepared wire its ruin away but the attacks did not succeed. During the day Batteries fired 40 R.G.F. per hour at intervals into POZIERES. It was expected that the ANZAC DIVISION would attack this place to-morrow morning, but the operation was postponed. S.C.	Appendix 4
	22/7/16		Batteries interned to fire into POZIERES during the day & reached the village between R.34.a.2.3 & the BAPAUME ROAD. Ammunition being carried up to Bty – Guns are frequently running out of action with buffer trouble – The Cable down still to hostile's Spring D & that – Old & prob. strained as put into runs when they – D.T.O.-N.-S.C.	
	23/7/16	12.30 AM	Zero – In an attack by Australian Div'n on POZIERES from S.E. – my Batteries A.B.C.D assist with Barrages – C. Battery moves to 40" Div." which is also carrying out an attack on left of AUSTRALIAN Division – Both attacks are successful – Australians from trenches & immediate vicinity. The latter part of day & night was spent – Batteries were preparing for a (counter attack) from ?. N. S.C.	Appendix 5

WAR DIARY or INTELLIGENCE SUMMARY

Army Form C. 2118.

Place	Date	Hour	Summary of Events and Information	Remarks and references to Appendices
As before	24/7/16		Aeroplane attacks having been pretty successful the morning is fairly quiet - but enemy shell POZIÈRES & Batteries are employed bombing N.G. POZIÈRES and keeping a look out for counter-attacks, which are expected but/are nothing so.	
	25/7/16		A good Reconnaissance was made by Capt. BARRY & Lieut DAVID of B Battery into POZIÈRES to find an O.P. - Other Officers of my Brigade also brought up but the Barrage is too heavy. All S.O.S Signal reported at O.A.8 p.m. but/none answered by	
	26/7/16		The above Reconnaissance was carried out to-day. Quiet during the morning except for the shelling of POZIÈRES - "A" Battery is stated at in desp[atches]. 4 S.W. Div 4 (cont.) a counter-attack. Re-issued Barrages at 6 night. No change of our line to Day &c	Appendix 6
	27/7/16		2nd LIEUT LOADER 'C'Battery made a useful reconnaissance in the early hours this morning into POZIÈRES - shelling of POZIÈRES by the enemy continues. My howitzers retaliate on trenches at R.34.d. at 6.30 p.m. &c	
	28/7/16		A fairly quiet day in the Batteries. POZIÈRES has heavily shelled Orders received for an attack on German Positions N x N.E. of POZIÈRES &c	
	29/7/16		Attack by our Infantry, Zero at 12.15 a.m - My Brigade co-operates in accordance with attached Orders (Appendix 7). Attacks not very successful on the right. On the left we held our own. Reports state we held only so far as R.33.d.8.7 & R.34.a.8.9., R.34.c.4.4 & 2.7.- Gas Alert warned at 8.30 p.m. but nothing happened. Counter attack reported at 9 p.m. but.	Appendix 7

Army Form C. 2118.

WAR DIARY
or
INTELLIGENCE SUMMARY
(Erase heading not required.)

Instructions regarding War Diaries and Intelligence Summaries are contained in F.S. Regs., Part II. and the Staff Manual respectively. Title Pages will be prepared in manuscript.

Place	Date	Hour	Summary of Events and Information	Remarks and references to Appendices
As before	28/7/16		but it does not materialise. 2C/	
"	30/7/16		During the day the Batteries were employed in bombarding at intervals the German System J Trenches N and N.E. of POZIERES. From 9 p.m. onwards "C" Battery took on a slow & these Trenches & fired all night. One of the guns endure. 2C/	
	31/7/16		The above fire continued up to 4.30 a.m. when it appeared — from 9 p.m. to 4.30 a.m. 1100 rounds were fired — from daylight till dark the Howitzer Battery used my (D Battery) fired any hour on the System J Trenches (N & N.E of POZIERES) - D.245 was placed tactically under my command and employed the same trenches firing 750 rounds between daylight and dark. 2C/	

E Cloete
Col R.A.
Cdy 111 Bde R.F.A.

25th Divisional Artillery.

111th BRIGADE.

ROYAL FIELD ARTILLERY

AUGUST 1 9 1 6

F 258

To/
Staff Captain
25th Div. R.A.

Herewith War Diary Vol XII
from 1st to 31st of August
and Appendix I to 6.

31-8-16

Thompson Major Commanding
111th Bde R.F.A.

Army Form C. 2118.

WAR DIARY
or
INTELLIGENCE SUMMARY
(Erase heading not required.)

Vol XII 111 R.F.A Vol 11

Place	Date	Hour	Summary of Events and Information	Remarks and references to Appendices
Guns in action W. OVILLERS	1.8.16		No Infantry attacks took place to-day. Batteries employed in Barrages in the morning & again at night on Trenches in R.34.a and d. Retaliation by enemy was feeble — Fine warm weather 2.C	
	2.8.16		Ordinary Barrage by 18 Batteries during early hours of the morning. No Infantry operations 2.C.	
	3.8.16		Ordinary Barrages during the day and registrations by 18 Batteries. The "Ration Trench" (X.3.b.5.7 — R.39.a.0.3) at 11 p.m. the 12th Bde Br made an attack in accordance with attached Orders — (Appendix 1) Only the howitzer Battery of the Brigade took part. Hot weather — The attack by 12th Div continued with successful results — At 7.15 a.m. "D" Battery F.O.O. reports retaliation by Artillery weak by Infantry but difficult to get owing to wires being broken. "D" Battery opens fire to assist in the capture of trench in R.33.c.	App. 1.
	4.8.16		Reconnaisance made yesterday by Capt. BARRY for important in X.9 (intended to-day with my 2 F.O.B's) & BIRMAN (F.O.O 25th N. Div. Art) Results of attacks yesterday successful — At 9/5 in ANZACS made an attack on Trench club NE of POZIERES and 7/11 the 12th Div also Appendix. attack NW of POZIERES assisted by Barrages by my Batteries. No information as to the nature of the attacks by 12. midnight. 2.C	App. 2.
	5.8.16		O.G.1 & O.G.2 have been taken by the ANZACS. Batteries during the day fire on trenches near MOUQUET FARM. "D" Battery fires THERMITE (Incendiary) Shell into Trench in R.33.c and at night at (source) LITE. Registration by Batteries in the afternoon. Barrages at night on R.33.a.8.1. to R.34.a.0.2. — Quiet night. Fine and warm 2.C	

Army Form C. 2118.

WAR DIARY or INTELLIGENCE SUMMARY

(Erase heading not required.)

Place	Date	Hour	Summary of Events and Information	Remarks and references to Appendices
Guns in positions as before	6.8.16		Batteries Barrage throughout the night & rounds fired every hour on tracks leading to PORCELETTE. Capt. BARRY makes a Reconnaissance towards X.15.b & X.16.d with a view to finding position to enfilade Trenches in X.31.a & X.31.c. Quiet day. Barrages at night as previous night. S.C. B? ADDISON. A Battery men? were under heavy fire. Near an explosion Bomb Dump	
"	7.8.16		Nothing special to record — No special operations — Batteries occupied in barraging in the neighbourhood of MOUQUET FARM. S.C.	
	8.8.16		During the day Batteries registered with air Aeroplane on Trench R.33.c.4.5. to R.33.d.8.1. — The registration appears satisfactory according to results given by the observer.	Appendix 3
		9.23. p.m.	The Australians & 12th Division made small attacks — and my Brigade cooperates in accordance with Orders attached S.C.	
	9.8.16		Barrages by the Brigade during early hours of the morning — Attack by Australians successful but 12th Div? not to successful. Barraging appears satisfactory in preparation for an attack S.C.	
	10.8.16		Australians & 12th Div? do ditto. 111th Brigade cooperates Australians & 12th Div? intensive their attack from midnight to 4.30.a.m. — Attacks both successful — at 10 p.m. — Nothing special to report —	Appendix 4
	11.8.16		Quiet day.	
	12.8.16		At 10.30 p.m. Australians & 12th Div? intensive their attacks — Batteries of 111th Brigade co-operate in accordance with attached Orders —	Appendix 5
	13.8.16		Australians & 12th Div? have (attained) their objectives — Quiet morning but Heavy firing by the enemy in the afternoon — Counter attack by Germans at 10 p.m. — S.O.S. was reported to us & Batteries open fire just at once but our Infantry are driven out & reported the trenches (captured the previous night)	

WAR DIARY or INTELLIGENCE SUMMARY

Army Form C. 2118

Place	Date	Hour	Summary of Events and Information	Remarks and references to Appendices
As before	14/8/16		A great deal of German activity during the morning. Our counterattack at 5.15.a.m was unsuccessful. Batteries did a good deal of firing. Quieter in the afternoon. 2nd LIEUT. LOWDER, "E" Battery reconnoitred the wire in X.2.a on the 70yds are aiming or information about it. The Australians & 48th Divn. continued their offensive. Batteries barrage from 10.30 p.m onwards.	Appendix 6
"	15/8/16		Nothing much done and there is no change in the situation. A quiet day on the whole &c. The usual barrage at midnight &c	
	16/8/16		A quiet day – during the night Batteries fired (intermittently from 8.55 p.m to 4.a.m on X.2.b & R.32.d – 2c	
	17/8/16		Nothing of importance to report. Batteries again fired (intermittently from 9.p.m to 4.15.a.m on 18½ on X.2.b & 32.d – 2c	
	18/8/16		Operations this evening by 48th Divn. – B. Battery ouput 14 3rd Infantry Brigade & comes under his orders. The Australians also intimate their intention at 9.p.m. – The 111th Bde is employed to keep down hostile fire from + to support hostile targets in R.P.I.d. – The Artillery barrage is reported by 143rd Inf. Brigade to have been very good. Capt. BARRY. B. Battery remains with 9.0. & 1423 J.B. during the operation &c	
	19/8/16		Operations last night reported to have been successful and a good deal of ground has been gained in X.2.a & X.2.b. Nothing of importance occurred yesterday. Capt. SHEAD. C. Battery was wounded yesterday in both thighs, it is thought by a short from one of our own 60 P.dr &c	

WAR DIARY or INTELLIGENCE SUMMARY

Army Form C.2118.

Place	Date	Hour	Summary of Events and Information	Remarks and references to Appendices
In action as before	20/8/16		Nothing special to record – B¹. ADDISON "A" Battery is awarded the Military Medal for his work on the 6ᵗʰ previously recorded. Maj. Gen. JACOB II Corp. Commander inspects A & D Batteries but has no time to go to C & D Batteries – He is extremely complimentary to us all on our work. Batteries Registered Trenches in X16 & R31d. Recce as the usual night fruinge.	
	21/8/16		Nothing of importance to report during the day. At 6 p.m the 48ᵗʰ Division made an attack on German Front Line & Support Trenches R32c. R31d and X16 & X1a – ⟨⟩ supported by fire from their Brigade & by our Batteries 2/	
	22/8/16		Attack last night & this morning early successful – a few dead & wounded Germans. Barrage appears to have been very good – one Infantry officer into German Trenches with few casualties – Capt. VINCENT from 112ᵗʰ Brigade succeeds Capt. SHEAD in command "C" Battery. Night firing as usual. A Counter-attack reported at 9.45 p.m. 2/	
	23/8/16	3 p.m.	48ᵗʰ Division continued the offensive and attempted to take R32c.31. – X2a75 but very successful – Batteries assisted with a Barrage –. The usual night	
	24/8/16		fruinge. Registering in the morning. A very successful attack by 25ᵗʰ Division at 4.10 p.m. – Practically all objectives gained in R31c and d – Artillery Barrage reported to be very good – 105 prisoners and many Germans killed – Night firing made as usual. 9c	

WAR DIARY or INTELLIGENCE SUMMARY

Army Form C. 2118.

Place	Date	Hour	Summary of Events and Information	Remarks and references to Appendices
In action as before.	25/8/16		The French (HINDENBURG) taken yesterday is being consolidated. The Germans shelled it a great deal during the day and very heavily about 7 p.m. — Counter attack reported. S.O.S. signals but not confirmed — however the fire of the Brigade and the RFA 2/5 - WF Div Artillery, as well as the fire of 2 other Divisions & Corps Heavy Artillery, was turned on. So counter attack or no counter attack the Germans must have had a bad time — must have had much attention — must have suffered much. Congratulatory messages received fr. B.G.R.A. on valuable information received from Artillery Cyprinks yesterday — also my attention letter from Corps & Divisional Commanders, &c.	
"	26/8/16		At 8 a.m. Germans are reported to be massing for a counter attack on the Australians who last night took R Trench [R.33.a.7.7 to R.33.b.6.2]. NW of MOUQUET FARM and the enemy's attack did not develop. The Batteries assisted in stopping any attempt at a counter attack — Between 6 & 8 p.m. various rumours were current of a counter attack on HINDENBURG TRENCH. Germans were seen NW of Trs & engaged by my Batteries — a very heavy Barrage was put up by the Germans on HINDENBURG TRENCH & we retaliated — nothing developed — &c.	
	27/8/16		Quiet morning — An attack was made in the evening at 7p.m. by 48th Bat on Trenches in R32.c.d. As far as can be ascertained this attack was mostly successful — Our Batteries barraged successfully &c	

Army Form C.2118.

WAR DIARY
or
INTELLIGENCE SUMMARY

(Erase heading not required.)

Instructions regarding War Diaries and Intelligence Summaries are contained in F.S. Regs., Part II. and the Staff Manual respectively. Title Pages will be prepared in manuscript.

Place	Date	Hour	Summary of Events and Information	Remarks and references to Appendices
Contay	28/9/16		Batteries registering. Major McLELLAN has a difficult task with his registration but accomplishes it successfully. In the afternoon at 4 p.m. the 7th Infantry Brigade made an attack in Area R31a and c. A Battery (Major McLELLAN) successfully put up its barrage. Unfortunately the attack does not meet with the success it deserves &c.	
	29/9/16		Quiet morning. Thunderstorm in the afternoon. Registration by A Batteries A & B. New MOUQUET FARM (inaccurately) difficult. Attacked by Australians on MOUQUET FARM & trenches round it at 11/5 a.m. A & B Batteries assist with a Barrage. No issual night firing &c.	
	30/9/16		The ANZACS appear to have gained their objectives last night and lost them again. My Batteries register their fire at –alarms. Very stormy morning. Batteries fire at Germans between 7 a.m. & 9 a.m. in R21.c.82. and appear to have dispersed them successfully with some casualties. Quiet. A very wet day. No usual night firing &c.	
	3/10/16		Very quiet morning. Nothing to record to day &c.	

E Chester Colonel
Cmd. 111 Inf. Bde. R.F.A.

SECRET. *Appendix I* Copy. No. 2

25th DIVISIONAL ARTILLERY OPERATION ORDER No.42.

3rd August, 1916.

Reference Trench Map
LA BOISSELLE. 1/5,000.

1. During night August 3rd/4th, the 12th Division will attack the German trenches on the line X 3 a 9 5, X 3 a 5 5, X 3 a 4 3, X 3 a 2 3, X 3 a 2 0.
   The above line will be consolidated, and connected with X 3 c 17.

2. The attack will take place at an hour, Zero, which will be (11 pm) notified later.

3. The attack will be preceded by an Artillery preparation of heavy and field artillery, and heavy and medium Trench Mortar Batteries, on the points to be attacked, and all the enemy's strong points and communication trenches.
   This preparation will consist of both steady artillery fire beforehand, and also of intense bursts of fire at irregular intervals up to the moment of attack.
   At the hour Zero an intense bombardment will be opened on the line to be attacked.
   At Zero + 5 minutes the bulk of the artillery will lift on to and beyond line X 2 b 2 0 - 6 2 - 9 0 - 9 4, X 3 a 9 9, R 33 d 7 8 (5th AVENUE after Pt.90.).
   At Zero plus 6 minutes the remainder of the artillery will lift similarly from the line to be attacked to the same line named in the preceding paragraph

4. The attacking Infantry will move forward as far as possible from their assembly positions, under the artillery barrage, and will attack when it lifts.

5. At Zero + 6 minutes a smoke barrage will be fired on X 2 b 9 0, X 2 b 6 2; to protect the left flank of the Infantry attack.
   This smoke barrage will continue for one hour.

6. The 25th Divisional Artillery will fire as follows:-
   From 0.0. to 0.6.
   18 pr batteries of 110th Brigade and of 112th Brigade will barrage strong point system from S.E. corner X 3 a 3025 to X 2 b 9027 and all trenches running from N.W. to S.E. in above work.
   Each Brigade will cover the whole system from X 3 a 3025 to X 2 b 9027. O.C. Brigades to allot one third of system to each Battery.
   Rate of fire 4 rounds per gun per minute.

   At 0.6.
   Fire of 18 pr batteries will lift.

   From 0.6. to 0.15.
   18 pr batteries will fire on trench from X 3 a 5070 to R 33 d 0 3.
   110th Brigade from X 3 a 5 7 to R 33 c 7505.
   112th "   " R 33 c 7505 to R 33 d 0 3.
   O.C. Brigades to allot one third of above lengths of trench to each Battery.
   Rate of fire 4 rounds per gun per minute.

   From 0.15. to 1.15.
   As from 0.6 to 0.15.
   Rate of fire 1 round per gun per minute

-2-

From 1.15 onwards. Fire to be continued at slow rate until G.O.C. 12th Division notifies that such fire is no longer required.

For all tasks 18 pdr. batteries will fire H.E. and shrapnel in proportion of 1 to 3.

Howitzer batteries.

From 0.0 to 0.15. Howitzer Batteries of 110th, 111th, & 112th Brigades will fire on trench from:
X 3 a 5 7   to R 33 d 0 3.
D/110 will fire on trench from X 3 a 5 7 to X 3 a 6590.
D/111 "   "   "   "   "   " X 3 a 6590 " R 33 c 8515.
D/112 "   "   "   "   "   " R 33 c 8515" R 33 d 0 3.
Rate of fire 2 rounds per How. per minute.

From 0.15 to 1.15. Howitzer Batteries will fire as from 0.0 to 0.15.
Rate of fire 1 round per How. per minute.

From 1.15 onwards. Fire of howitzers will be continued at a slow rate until the G.O.C. 12th Division notifies that such fire is no longer required.

[handwritten margin note: 1 R'd per gun per 2 minutes]

B.K. Kirwan
Major, R.A.
Bde Major, 25th Divl. Artillery.

Issued at 3.45 p.m.

Copies to:
No. 1.   110th Bde. R.F.A.
   2.   111th Bde.   "
   3.   112th Bde.   "
   4.   D.A.C.
   5.   R.A. 2nd Corps.
   6.   2nd Australian Division.
   7.   12th Division 'G'.
   8.   12th Divl. Arty.

Appendix 2

Copy No. 2

S E C R E T

25th DIVISIONAL ARTILLERY OPERATION ORDER No. 43.

Reference Map LA BOISSELLE.
1/5,000.

1. The 2nd Australian Division will attack the trenches known as O.G.1. and O.G.2. from X 5 a 9 5 to R 34 a 9 1.
   The first objective is O.G.1.
   The second " is O.G.2.

2. The attack will take place at zero viz 9.15 p.m. August 4th.

3. Detail of troops for attack :-

    5th Aust. Inf. Bde. Objective X 5 a 9 5 to BAPAUME road at X 5 a 7 9 and TORR AVENUE up to point where it crosses tram line at X 5 b 0550.

    7th Aust. Inf. Bde.
       1st Objective   R 35 c 6 0 to R 34 d 7 7
       2nd "   R 35 c 8515 to R 34 b 6 0 ? 9
       The Windmill will be captured.

    6th Aust. Inf. Bde.
       1st Objective   R 34 d 7 7 to R 34 a 9 1
       2nd "   ? R 34 b 6 0 9 to R 34 b 1 2

4. At the same hour viz 9.15 p.m. on 4th August the 12th Division will continue their Offensive with the object of gaining the following points :-
   R 33 d 7 7 - 7 8 - 8 9 by the 36th Inf. Bde
   and points
   X 2 b 6 2 - 7 4 - 9 4

5. The 25th Divl. Artillery will support these attacks as follows :-
   The 111th Brigade will support the 12th Division with their 18 pdr. batteries.
   The 110th and 112th Brigades will support the ANZACS each Brigade with 10 guns.
   Fire to be as per attached table.

6. There will be no fire within 450 yards of O.G.2. after its capture, between 12 midnight and 12.45, to enable patrols to explore the ground in that area.

7. Hostile counter attack. In case of hostile counter attack, the existing S.O.S. Signal of three red rockets will be used, and in addition Red Very Lights will be fired in quick succession, in groups of three, along the front the enemy is attacking, whereupon the artillery will maintain a barrage 150 yards in front of O.G.2.
   In addition to the above, "Lights long green" will be carried (4 per platoon) and will be used occasionally to indicate the position of our troops to our artillery. Green lights are NOT S.O.S. Signals.

-2-

8. <u>Communication with aeroplanes.</u>

Green flares, in groups of three, lit one after the other (in a trench) are to be used by <u>all</u> Brigades, during daylight.

Each Battalion will light flares at the following fixed hours :-
    5 a.m.   11 a.m.   5 p.m.   8 p.m.

Each Company, or portion of a company, in O.G.2, will light flares at the above hours, in addition to the **Battalion Signal.**

The tin discs, ordered to be carried by each man, are to be tied on the back when it is desired to show the position of troops to our artillery behind, or to our aeroplanes.

[signature]

Issued at 7. p.m.

Major, R.A.
Bde Major, 25th Divl. Arty.

Copies to :
- No 1.   110th Bde. R.F.A.
- 2.   111th Bde. "
- 3.   112th Bde. "
- 4.   D.A.C.
- 5.   R.A. II Corps.
- 6.   2nd Australian Division "G".
- 7.   12th Division 'G'
- 8.   12th Divl. Artillery.

BDE.	TIME.	OBJECTIVE.	DETAILS.	AMMUNITION & RATES OF FIRE.	
111th Bde.	0.0. to 0.20.	Barrage from R 34 a 5 3.	10 18pr guns.	4 rounds per gun per minute.	H.E. & Shrapnel 1 to 3.
	0.20 to 0.30.	----ditto----	ditto	2 rounds per gun per minute.	"
	0.30 till notified that barrage no longer required.	----ditto----	ditto	1 round per battery per minute	"
	0.0. to 1 hour.	Road from MOUQUET FARM to R 33 b 5 5	D/110	150 rounds.	
112th Bde.	0.0. to 0.3.	Barrage R 34 a 5 3 to R 34 a 9 1.	10 18pr guns	4 rounds per gun per minute.	H.E. & Shrapnel 1 to 3.
	0.3 to 0.13.	R 34 a 5 3 to R 34 b 1 2.	"	----ditto----	"
	0.13 to 0.15.	R 34 a 5 3 to R 34 b 1½ 3.	"	----ditto----	"
	0.15 to 0.17.	R 34 a 5 3 to R 34 b 2 3½.	"	----ditto----	"
	0.17 to 0.20.	R 34 a 5 3 to R 34 b 3 3½.	"	----ditto----	"
	0.20 to 0.30	----ditto----	"	2 rounds per gun per minute.	"
	0.30 till notified that barrage will cease.	----ditto----	"	1 round per bty per minute.	"

UNIT.	TIME.	OBJECTIVE.	BATTERIES.	AMMUNITION & RATES OF FIRE.	
111th Bde. 9.15-to 9.20	0.0. to 0.5.	R 33 d 7 8 - R 33 d 2 6.	10 18pr guns.	4 rounds per gun per minute.	H.E. & Shrapnel 1 to 3.
9.20 to 9.30	0.5. to 0.15.	R 33 b 6 1 - R 33 a 8 1.	"	------ditto-----	"
9.30 to 10	0.15 to 0.45.	---ditto----	"	1 round per gun per minute.	"
	0.45	cease fire.			
	0.0. to 1 hour.	R 34 b 3 4 - R 34 b 8 6.	D/111.	150 rounds.	
	1 hour onwards.	---ditto----	"	60 rounds per hour.	

Appendix 3

SECRET.   Copy No....

25th DIVISIONAL ARTILLERY OPERATION ORDER No. 44.

                                                    8th August, 1916.
                        ---------ooOoo---------

Reference 1/5000
Map. LA BOISSELLE.

1. On night August 8th/9th, the 4th Australian Division will attack the German defences on the line R.34.b.2.4.- R.34.a.8.3.- ?.4. - 5.3. - 1.2., R.33.d.9.9. - R.33.d.8.9.inclusive.

2. The 12th Division will co-operate in this attack, and capture the German defences about R.33.d.7.8., obtaining connection with the 4th Australian Division at R.33.d.8.9.

3. The attack will be preceded by an effective Heavy and Field Artillery bombardment all day.
   At 9.20.p.m. all available Field Artillery will open an intense bombardment on the objectives to be attacked, and the Infantry will push forward towards them under its protection.
   At 9.23 p.m. the bombardment will lift, and the Infantry will assault.

4. Red flares will indicate the position of 12th Division Infantry.

5. The fire of 25th Divisional Artillery will be as below:-
   The 110th Brigade will detail D/110 to fire one round per howitzer per minute on the area between R.27.d.1.2 and R.33.b.2.9. commencing at 9.20.p.m., and ceasing fire at 9.50.p.m.
   The 111th Brigade will detail all 18 pr guns to barrage the line joining the points R.33.b.3.3. - 5.5. - R.34.a.3.8. commencing 9.20.p.m., three rounds per gun per minute.
   At 9.24.p.m. rate of fire to be reduced to one round per gun per minute.
   From 9.50.p.m. four 18 pr guns only will continue this barrage. Rate of fire reduced to one round per battery per minute.
   The 112th Brigade will detail two 18 pr guns to enfilade the road from R.33.b.8.0. to R.33.b.7.2. commencing at 9.15.p.m. Rate of fire three rounds per gun per minute.
   At 9.25.p.m. fire to be lifted to enfilade road from R.33.b.5.5. up to MOUQUET FARM.
   112th Brigade will also detail six guns to barrage the line R.33.b.3.3. - 5.5. - R.34.a.3.8. commencing at 9-50.p.m. Rate of fire 120 rounds per hour.
   Ammunition H.E. and Shrapnel 1 to 3.

                                               Major. R.A.
                                      Brigade Major, 25th Divl Arty.

Issued at 7.p.m.
   Copies to
      O.C.110 Brigade.
      O.C.111th   "
      O.C.112th   "
      O.C.25th D.A.C.
      R.A. 2nd Corps.
      12th Division. G.
         "   "   Arty.
      4th Australian Divn. G.

SECRET.   Appendix 4   Copy No. 7

25th DIVISIONAL ARTILLERY OPERATION ORDER No. 45.

9th August, 1916.

Reference 1/5000
Map LA BOISSELLE.

1. On night August 9th/10th, the 4th Australian Division will continue their operation to complete the capture of the line R 34 b 2 4 – R 34 a 8 3 – 5 3 – 1 2 – R 33 d 8 9 – 7 8 – 7 7.
   The 12th Division will, at the same hour, make a bombing attack up RATION TRENCH to R 33 d 7 7 to join hands with the 4th Australian Division at this point.
   The attack will take place at Zero, viz, midnight on 9th/10th August.

2. The 25th Divisional Artillery will cooperate as follows:-

   The 110th Brigade will detail one 18 pr battery to put bursts of fire at irregular intervals on the line R 28 c 0 4 – 3 6 – 6 6 – 9 5 between the hours of 9.p.m. and 4-30.a.m. Ammunition 30 rounds per hour.   3 Shrapnel to 1 H.E.

   The 111th Brigade will detail one 18 pr battery to barrage the line R 33 b 5 5 to R 34 a 3 8.
   Fire to commence at Zero.
   Rate of fire:-   Zero to plus 5.   Three rounds per gun per minute.
                    Plus 5 to plus 30.   One round "   "   "   "
                    Plus 30 onwards.   One round per battery per minute.
   Three rounds shrapnel to one H.E.

   112th Brigade will detail one 18 pr battery to fire bursts at irregular intervals between the hours of 9.p.m. and 4-30.a.m., on the trenches joining the points R 27 d 1 2 – 4 2 – 3 1 and R 33 b 5 9 also between R 27 d 4 2 – 9 4.
   Ammunition 30 rounds per hour.   3 Shrapnel to 1 H.E.

                                          Brigadier-General.
                                Commanding 25th Divisional Arty.

Issued at 7.p.m.
Copies to:-
O.C. 110th Brigade.
O.C. 111th   "
O.C. 112th   "
O.C. 25th D.A.C.
O.C. 12th Division. G.
2nd Corps. R. A.
12th Div'l Arty.
2nd Australian Div'n Arty.
4th Australian Div'n G.
Staff Captain 25th D.A.

Appendix 5

SECRET   Copy No. 2

25th DIVISIONAL ARTILLERY OPERATION ORDER No. 46.

12th August 1916.

Reference Trench
Map 1/5,000.

1. The offensive will be continued to-night August 12th/13th at Zero, which will be at 10.30 p.m.

2. The objectives of 4th Australian Division are :-
R. 34. a. 3. 8. - R. 33. b. 5. 5. - R. 33. a. 8. 1. (inclusive).
The objectives of 12th Division are :-
R. 33. a. 8. 1. (exclusive) - R. 33. c. 1. 4. - X. 2. b. 9. 9. - 7. 8. - 4. 4. - 6. 2.
After capturing this line posts will be established at R. 32. d. 8. 1. - X. 2. b. 5. 9., X. 2. b. 4. 8. and X. 2. b. 0. 6.
The objective of 49th Division is X. 2. c. 3. 9.

3. The dividing line between 4th Australian Division and 12th Division will be the POZIERES - THIEPVAL road.

4. The attack will probably be assisted by a smoke barrage on selected points.

5. 25th Divisional Artillery will fire as in attached table.

6. ACKNOWLEDGE.

M. Duke.
Major, R.A.

Issued at 5 p.m.   Bde Major, 25th Divl. Artillery.

Copy to :-

No. 1. 110th Bde. R.F.A.
    2. 111th Bde.
    3. 112th Bde.
    4. D.A.C.
    5. R.A. 2nd Corps.
    6. 12th Divn. 'G'.
    7. R.A. 12th Divn.
    8. 4th Australian Division.
    9. Lahore Divl. Arty.
    10. 49th Division 'G'.

TIME TABLE for 18 pdr. guns. 25th DIVISIONAL ARTILLERY. Night August 12th/13th.

Unit.	Time.	Objective.		Rate of fire.
2 Batteries 112th Bde.	Zero to 0.3.	A.	X. 2. b. 4. - X. 2. b. 9. 9.	4 rounds per gun per minute.
2 " 112th "	0.3.to 0.7.	B.	X. 2. b. 5. 9. - R.32. d. 4. 3.	4 rounds per gun per minute.
1 Bty 112th Bde.	Zero to 0.5.	A.	X. 2. b. 9. 9. - R.33. c. 0. 2.	4 rounds per gun per minute
3 Batteries 110th Bde.	" " " "	A.	R.33. c. 0. 2. to R.33.c.4555	----ditto----
3 " 111th "	" " " "	A.	R.33.c.4565 to R.33. 8. 1.	----ditto----
1 Bty 112th Bde.	0.5. to 0.7.	B.	R.32. d. 4. 3. - R.32. d. 5262	4 rounds per gun per minute
3 Batteries 110th Bde.	" " " "	B.	R.32. d. 5262 - R.32. b. 9015	----ditto----
3 Batteries 111th Bde.	" " " "	B.	R.32. b. 9015 - R.33. 8. 5. 4.	----ditto----
All Batteries	0.7 to 0.30	Objectives B.		2 rounds per gun per minute
At 0.30 112th Brigade will lift from Point A. 2. b. 5. 9. as below. After 0.30 no fire to be South of R.32.d.4.3.				
112th Bde.	0.30 to 1 hour.	R.32. d. 4. 3. to R.32. d. 6. 8.		1 round per gun per minute
110th & 111th Bdes.	0.30 to 1 hour.	Objectives B.		----ditto----
All Batteries	1 hour to 1.30	As for 0.30 to 1 hour.		½ round per gun per minute

TIME TABLE for 4.5" Hows. 25th DIVISIONAL ARTILLERY. Night August 12th/13th.

Unit.	Time.	Objective.	Rate of fire.
D/110	Zero to 0.15	X. 2. a. 5. 6. X. 2. a. 6. 5.	2 rounds per How. per minute
D/111	–do–	X.2.a.7.3.–R.32.c.9.1.–R.32.c.5505	–do–
D/112	–do–	R.32.c.5.6. R.32.c.6.6. R.32.c.6.5.	–do–
All How Batteries	0.15 to 0.45	As for zero to 0.15	1 round per How. per minute

Appendix 6

Copy No. 2

25th DIVISIONAL ARTILLERY OPERATION ORDER No. 47.

Reference Trench Map
1/5,000.

14th August 1916.

1. The 4th Australian Division and 48th Division will resume the offensive tonight, August 14th/15th, at zero hour, which will be 10 p.m.

2. The objectives of 4th Australian Division (13th Australian Infantry Brigade) will be :— R. 28. c. 9. 5. — 6. 6. — 3. 6. — 2. 4. — 0. 3. — 0. 4.
R. 27. d. 9. 4. — 7. 3. — 9. 1.
R. 33. b. 4. 8.   R. 33. a. 8. 1.

The objectives of 48th Division will be :—
(a) X. 2. b. 6. 2.   X. 2. b. 4. 4. 74. 55.
(b) *secure point 81 in R. 33.a, and open communication with R.33.d.2.6*

3. Strong points will be established at R.28.c.9.5., R.27.d.7.3. — 9. 1. and near R.33.b.4.8.

4. The 25th Divisional Artillery will fire as in attached table.

5. Acknowledge.

Major, R.A.
Bde Major, 25th Divl. Artillery

Issued at 8.50/pm.

Copies to :—

No. 1. 110th Bde. R.F.A.
2. 111th Bde.   "
3. 112th Bde.   "
4. D.A.C.
5. R.A. 2nd Corps.
6. 48th Divn. 'G'
7. 48th Divl. Arty.
8. 4th Australian Divn. 'G'
9. Lahore Artillery.

THE R.A. 25th DIVISIONAL ARTILLERY Night 14th/15th August 1916.

Unit.	Time.	Objective.	Rate of fire.
111th Brigade 2 18 pdr.batteries	Zero onwards.	R.32.d.0.3. - 2.5. - 2.5.-6.9.	50 rds per bty per hour till ordered to stop.
111th Brigade 1 18 pdr. battery.	"	R.32.d.6.9.- R.33.a.0025	-ditto-
112th Brigade 1 18 pdr.battery.	"	R.33.a.0025 - R.33.a.4.4.	-ditto-
110th Brigade 3 18 pdr.batteries	Zero to 0.3.	R.33.a.4.4.- R.33.a.9.6.	4 rds per gun per minute.
112th Brigade 2 18 pdr.batteries	" " "	R.33.a.9.6.- R.33.b.2.7.	-ditto-
110th Brigade 3 18 pdr.batteries	0.3. to 0.5.	R.33.a.4.4. direct to R.33.a.7.7. direct to R.33.a.8.9.	4 rds per gun per minute.
112th Brigade 2 18 pdr.batteries	" " "	R.33.a.8.9. direct to R.27.d.1.2.	-ditto-
110th Brigade 3 18 pdr. batteries	0.5. to 0.7.	R.33.a.4.4. direct to R.33.a.7.7. direct to R.27.c.8.1.	4 rds per gun per minute.
112th Brigade 2 18 pdr.batteries	" " "	R.27.c.8.1. direct to R.27.d.0.5.	-ditto-

FIRE TABLE 25th DIVISIONAL ARTILLERY, Night 14th/15th.

Page 2.

Unit.	Time.	Objective.	Rate of fire.
110th Brigade 3 18 pdr. batteries	0.7. to 0.30	As for 0.5. to 0.7.	2 rds per gun per minute.
112th Brigade 2 18 pdr. batteries	" " "	As for 0.5. to 0.7.	–ditto–
110th Brigade 318 pdr. batteries & 112th Brigade 2 18 pdr. batteries	0.30 to 1 hour.	As for 0.5. to 0.7.	1 round per gun per minute.
110th Brigade 3 18 pdr. batteries & 112th Brigade 2 18 pdr. batteries	1 hour to 1 hr.30.	As for 0.5. to 0.7.	1 round per gun per 2 minutes.
111th Brigade 'D' Battery (Hows.)	Zero onwards.	R.32.d.0.0.3., 1.2.2.3, R.33.c.4.4, 5.4.	50 rounds per hour till ordered to stop..

25th. DIVISION

ARTILLERY

111th. BRIGADE   R. F. A.

25th. DIVISIONAL   ARTILLERY

S E P T E M B E R   1 9 1 6.

F 727.

To/
Staff Captain
25th Div

Herewith War Diary of 111th
Bde for Sept.

Oct 1.

Champion - Adjt
111th Bde R.F.A

WAR DIARY
or
INTELLIGENCE SUMMARY.
(Erase heading not required.)

Vol XIII
111 RFA

Place	Date	Hour	Summary of Events and Information	Remarks and references to Appendices
In action S.W. of OVILLERS	1/9/16		Not much firing during the day by Batteries. Ammunition being a bit short. Night firing on communication & other trenches, also on Tracks — 100 Rds per Battery per hour. Less 1 B/A⁹ at 10 p.m. than usual. 10 in action but guns all getting worse. &c	
"	2/9/16		Batteries occupied in registering trenches for future operation. A Battery on several occasions during the day sniped Germans in trench R 31 d 4 8 Vag¹ and in NUNDWERK. No heavy hostile fire. &c	
"	3/9/16	5.10 am	Attack by 25th Div. on trenches No 9 LEIPZIG SALIENT — Otherwise, to the North & East all Batteries employed trenches (Frontiers & Support) were made as co-operation. The attack was not successful. In the afternoon in support of the 8th Div. attack. A Battery did good work sniping Germans R 31 b 5.9 - 7.8 & thin trench to neighbourhood of the Apples Trees. Germans rifle seen & sniped by all batteries during the day. Night firing 35 Rounds per Brig'de per hour rapid lading trench P 31 a 9.4 - 3.12.06 &c	
"	4/9/16		B Battery registered trenches in R 32 b & 33 a. Observation done from R 31 a 90 - a difficult place to keep a view firing but fortunately there is little protective fire LIEUT PAGE transferred to an Anti Aircraft Section. LIEUT. DAVID. D.C.H. 25. May 2 B'OT PAGE transferred to an Anti Aircraft Section. Night firing 30 Rds. Shots back in R 32 (central to be full of Germans & dugouts) &c	
"	5/9/16		Few hours communication trench to hospitals &c. Batteries fire during the day on communication trenches NORTHERN AL where considerable movement has been reported. Registration by A C & D Batteries of trenches in R 32 b & R 33 a. At 12.10 p.m two Batteries in to trench. Band? about R 92 b 21 where Germans were spotted yesterday by LIEUT C.H. DAVID. Later in the evening A Battery assisted ANZACS by firing in enfilade on trench running through R 2 & R.E. 95 a trench 40 Rds per hour. Movements East night HINDURBURG through R 2 & R.E. also into WINDWERN. &c	

Army Form C. 2118.

WAR DIARY
or
INTELLIGENCE SUMMARY
(Erase heading not required.)

Instructions regarding War Diaries and Intelligence Summaries are contained in F. S. Regs., Part II. and the Staff Manual respectively. Title pages will be prepared in manuscript.

Place	Date	Hour	Summary of Events and Information	Remarks and references to Appendices
As before	6/9/16		Howitzers during the day fired at the WELLS Bank in R32 central b - Also at 12.30 p.m. and again between 2.40 p.m. & 3.30 p.m. were turned on to WUNDWERK in retaliation for enemy's shelling. This was done at the request of the Infantry. 18 Pr Batteries sniped Germans at R21.c.2.6 & R26.c.7. & R32.central. - B battery also registered 31.a.4.5. & c & D Batteries JOSEPH. FRENCH. - Nightfiring 20 rounds an hour on 31.6.60 to 32.a.2.6. At 7.15 p.m. D Battery Howitzers observed an Ascow Winker Call & shot at R14 d 25.60 (2 Motor cars) - The Battery got quickly going S.E.	
"	7/9/16		At 3.15 a.m. S.O.S reported. - Batteries at once turned on to Counter-attack Barrages in R31a.b & the Counter attack developed. Howitzers also fired into CORCELETTE - During the day D Battery fired at 2 aeroplanes (all targets. - Other Batteries re-registered & ringed Germans at R31.b.4.5. & R21.c.2.7 & R2.b.6.15.00. - Nightfiring 20 Rds an hour. R31.6.60 - R32.a.2.6. SE	
"	8/9/16		At 7.40 a.m. Germans shelled the neighborhood of MOUQUET. FARM. - Our Batteries assisted by staffing & enfilading Trenches in R7.c.c. d. - Howitzers during the day put several Salvoes into CORCELETTE - working parties were sniped by A/13 at R31.d.4.8. - The 25th Divl. Artl. Corps not yet actual at 8.30 p.m. - This Brigade remains in its positions as being preparing to going to wagon lines which are continually shelled - S.C.	
As before but batteries out of action	9/9/16		Batteries are no longer in action. The work of overhauling guns and equipment goes on S.C.	

WAR DIARY
or
INTELLIGENCE SUMMARY
(Erase heading not required.)

Place	Date	Hour	Summary of Events and Information	Remarks and references to Appendices
As before	10/9/16		Still out of action — Overhauling B guns and equipment – 2C	
"	11/9/16		Orders received to be in action again to-morrow morning – Guns buffers etc re-assembled – 2C	
"	12/9/16		In action again. Registration by all Batteries in view of future operations. 2C	
"	13/9/16		Further Registrations for future operations 2C	
"	14/9/16		All Batteries re-registering. All Batteries at 6.30 p.m. put-port (?) the 11" Division in an attack on WUNDWERK - Creeping Shooting but Barrage reported by Aeroplanes to be good - Enemy Infantry appear to have started before time. Several aircraft calls received between 7 p.m. & 7.30 p.m. and all within Range taken on by A & D Batteries 2C Staff Officer.	
"	15/9/16		S.O.S. call at 12.15 a.m. Batteries all put up a Barrage - No serious retaliation. Batteries all objective appear to be held — Aircraft (all at 9 a.m. taken on by D Battery. Other area calls taken up by Batteries during the morning. Retaliation at 12.50 p.m. by all Batteries put the shelling of our trenches. No night firing SC.	
"	16/9/16		Aeroplane targets taken on during the day — In two cases Aeroplane signals "mostly O.K." Nothing else to record SC	
"	17/9/16		many Aeroplane Targets engaged by all Batteries - At 6.45 p.m. to 7.30 p.m. all Batteries Barrage in R31.a & b & R25.d - Quiet night - 2C	

WAR DIARY or INTELLIGENCE SUMMARY

Army Form C. 2118.

Place	Date	Hour	Summary of Events and Information	Remarks and references to Appendices
As before	18/9/16		Too wet & misty for observation.	
	19/9/16		A good deal of movement observed. Very quiet day in consequence &c. Very quiet day in consequence. Batteries engaged about the ZOLLERN REDOUBT and N.W. of it. Batteries engaged parties of Germans in that neighbourhood. All O.C. Batteries took on hostile Battery in action in R.11.c. treated by Aeroplane. At 1 p.m. 3 Germans were seen on a Chalk Mound at R.27.b.17 - Engaged by "D" Battery - All 3 Germans pushed over. 2. Targets given by Aeroplane engaged in the evening - No night firing &c.	
	20/9/16		Registrations by Batteries of Trenches in R.31 a & b had to be stopped owing to our Infantry having made a small advance - No Area calls to-day - Ammunition expenditure limited to 166 Rounds per Brigade daily - No night firing &c.	
	21/9/16		Very quiet day. Limited amount of ammunition. Batteries do little firing. At night - 3 Batteries fire at enemy Batteries in R.21 - 2 c.	
	22/9/16		Orders received for registration to be carried out on Trenches in R.2 b & c. R.20d & R.2 o.c. - All Batteries take on several Aeroplane Targets in R.15 a & e and N.10d. Reconnoitring in new O.P.'s by B.O.'s - At 8.15. S.O.S reported at R.33 a 54 - Batteries fired on Barrage Lines - Enemy's bombs attack repulsed &c.	
	23/9/16		Registration of ZOLLERN, SCHWABEN, BULGAR Trenches - Also MARTINS LANE & MIDWAY L, NE.	
	24/9/16		Further registration of above Trenches - Visibility till the afternoon - Three Area calls responded to by all Batteries - No night firing &c.	

WAR DIARY / INTELLIGENCE SUMMARY

Army Form C. 2118.

Place	Date	Hour	Summary of Events and Information	Remarks and references to Appendices
~~Stuff~~ as before	25/9/16		Quiet morning. Further Registration by Batteries - and a Barrage fired in the afternoon. No night firing.	
	26/9/16		Operations on a large scale by 18th, 4th & Canadian Divisions - this Brigade supported the attack of 18th Division - all Batteries fired a Barrage from 12.35 p.m. Of Batteries which were received (lasted till 7 p.m. during which firing, the Brigade fired 4359 Rounds B.S.M. BATCHELOR ~~was~~ of "B" Battery 111th Brigade is awarded the Military X for devotion to duty on several occasions when the wagon lines were shelled, and on one occasion where his lorry & ammunition wagons was shelled. During the night, the 13th fired 1616 & Rounds 8 Rounds per Bdr. into R.20.c. and d.-9e.	
	27/9/16		Batteries fired at Aeroplane Targets - at 4.30 p.m. I received orders that 18th Divn. would resume attack on SCHWABEN REDOUBT at 5 a.m. got out Barrages but attack postponed. night firing 166 Rds per hour per Bn? (10th) into R.20 c 9 c.	
	28/9/16		The postponed attack on SCHWABEN REDOUBT. is resumed at 16 w Batteries fire a Barrage in R.26a. R.20 a.*b. & R.19 b. & d. - ~~respectfully~~ B.C.'s do reconnoitre for new positions about R.32 a & c. - The Batteries move into the new positions in R.32 c. during the night. No night firing 29/	
Ammunition in R.32c.	29/9/16		Batteries settled in new positions by 6.30 a.m. Very misty & no visibility & consequently no registration possible - Orders received to move Batteries by sending 6 mis & 6 mym nights. To cover 25th Div. Infantry, Positions are in X 3 c. b & d. S.O.S. reported at 9.30 p.m. Batteries increased rate on might firing duties in R.14 & R.15 2 c.	

Army Form C. 2118.

WAR DIARY
or
INTELLIGENCE SUMMARY
(Erase heading not required.)

Instructions regarding War Diaries and Intelligence Summaries are contained in F.S. Regs., Part II. and the Staff Manual respectively. Title Pages will be prepared in manuscript.

Place	Date	Hour	Summary of Events and Information	Remarks and references to Appendices
Guns in action in R3QC.	30/9/16		One Section J 29th Battery moved to new positions last night — Positions are in X3 b.b.9.d. — Rn move in in order that the 25th & a very crew German Infantry — At 6.50 a.m. there were a frantic attack on SCHWABEN REDOUBT — Batteries all of ourspire on the enemy way —	"SCHWABEN"
		4 p.m.	18th Division attack R20 & R27 — 19 at 99 — 69 — 4.9 — 3.9. All Batteries cooperate — Night firing. 30 RWS per Brigade.	

E Close
Col RA
Cd. 111 6th Bde RFA

25th. DIVISION
ARTILLERY

111th. BRIGADE R. F. A.

25th. DIVISIONAL ARTILLERY

OCTOBER 1916.

Ceased to exist Nov 1916

WAR DIARY / INTELLIGENCE SUMMARY

Army Form C. 2118.

111 Bde R.F.A. Vol 13

Place	Date	Hour	Summary of Events and Information	Remarks and references to Appendices
In action between POZIERES and OVILLERS	1/10/16		Relief of this brigade by 83rd Bde. R.F.A. 18th Divn. completed last night. 83rd Bde R.F.A. at 6 A.M. to-day. Brigade have moved to W.18.d.63. moves to OVILLERS. this brigade relieved and took over guns and positions from 2.H.3.Bde A.& H. Divn. last night. 9 A.M. this morning. Engaged aeroplane targets during day. Night firing on R.21.b.7.9. to R.21.b.9.4. 36 rounds per hour.	Ab.
	2.X.16		Relation of C.P's and registration prevented by low weather, mist and rain — night look out stations at OVILLERS manned by one officer from this brigade.	Ab
	3.X.16		Heavy rain and mist hindering much registration. Night firing. 18 pr. hostile from R.15.c.9.5 to R.15.d.3.1.6.H.H. 4.5 Howitzer Zollern Redt, Quid Hay GRANDCOURT, leaders F.R. BARRY 4th B Bty assumed command of brigade during absence of Col. Blockk H.R. who is acting I.R.G.	A.b.
	4.X.16		Quiet day. 1 P.M. Brigade fired barrage on enemy trenches, hostile seven minutes. Barrage B.21.6.34.65. Night firing 18 prs. 10 rounds an hour into GRANDCOURT. 15 pm 25 rounds an hour R.22.a.2.6. 4.5 H. to R.16.c.66. 3 HE. to 1 shrapnel.	M.
	5.X.16		Batteries engaged from aeroplane targets during day; about twenty target. Night firing:— 4.5 How. 10 rounds per battery at each to R.16.c.7.7. Ten rounds per hour into GRANDCOURT. 18 prs. fired on R.22.a.n.8.	Ab.
	6.X.16		Five aeroplane targets engaged by batteries: 15 to 30 rounds fired by each battery in answer to these. Howitzers fired at night into GRANDCOURT. 18 prs fired on R.22.b.5.6. to R.17.a.0.0. and searched roads in R.17.a.	Ab
	7.X.16	6PM	Quiet day. 5 Howitzer battery registered with aeroplane during morning on REGINA Trench afterwards firing two hundred rounds in same target. In afternoon same D battery heavily shelled with 5.9's. Two direct hits on gun pits and telephone dug-out buried by another direct hit. Shelling lasted 2½ hours. no casualties to men or material. S.O.I. signal by rockets near STUFF Redoubt, all batteries of this brigade fired into GRANDCOURT. 10 rounds per hour. 18 pr. when ordinary night firing was resumed at night. Howitzers fired until 4 P.M.	Ab. Ab ?

Army Form C. 2118.

111 Bde RFA

WAR DIARY
or
INTELLIGENCE SUMMARY
(Erase heading not required.)

Instructions regarding War Diaries and Intelligence Summaries are contained in F. S. Regs., Part II. and the Staff Manual respectively. Title Pages will be prepared in manuscript.

Place	Date	Hour	Summary of Events and Information	Remarks and references to Appendices
Batteries POZIERES & OVILLERS	8.X.16	4.50 PM	This brigade carried out attack of 3rd Canadian Division on REGINA Trench and eastwards. All 18 hr Howd (less 2nd J.O.M. with 2 firing trench) in barrage with seven lifts. Three minutes shrapnel to one Std. No trouble for infantry.	1/1
		5 P.M.	D Battery again heavily shelled. One gun pit blown in and gun actual destroyed. Shelling mostly of 5.9 shells. Lasted in two bursts for about 80 minutes. D Battery changes position during night 8/9 O.M.	
	9.X.16	12.35 PM	3 guns of A Bty, 2 guns of C Bty, out of action at J.O.M. 18 hrs of this brigade less 5 at J.O.M. supported attack of 10th Canadian Regt 7th Bde 3rd Dn to gain the remainder of STUFF REDOUBT and points just beyond. Three lifts in barrage. No trouble for infantry.	1/1
		6.15PM	S.O.S. received from Brigade Major on STUFF Redoubt. This brigade barrage until 6.45 PM and then resumed night firing. Barrage fired into GRANDCOURT during night and 12 hr 25 minutes per hour on R.22.a.4.8. R.16.c.6.3.	1/1
	10.X.16		A quiet day. Major G. R. MacKellar took over command of brigade from Captain F. R. Barry.	1/1
	11.X.16	2.30 PM	At 2.30 P.M. and again at 7 P.M. enemy opened very heavy fire on STUFF Redoubt. All batteries of this brigade replied and fired for nearly an hour on each occasion. No infantry action followed enemy barrage.	1/1
	12.X.16	3 P.M.	In afternoon at 3 P.M. enemy put heavy fire for an hour. At 6.45 P.M. S.O.S. signal on STUFF Redoubt. All batteries of this brigade were still firing when liaison officer with 74th and 76th Infy Bde's rang through by telephone another 'S.O.S.' just received from battalion. Germans attacked near STUFF Redoubt but were repulsed. Both attacks. One infantry report artillery fire "extremely accurate."	1/1
	13.X.16		C Battery shelled heavily all day with 7.7 + 4.20 Whizr averaging some 5.9 and now Emmy day shells were mostly from 7in guns and came in batches of a dozen every fifteen minutes. Two pits received direct hits and one howitzer in without damaging guns. Three dugouts also destroyed by direct hits but no casualties. 18 hrs fired 100 rounds during twenty minute during night into GRANDCOURT, MIRAUMONT and PETIT MIRAUMONT. Also at crossroads & H.Q. G.RAND COURT. { R.22.a.4.8. to R.16.c.6.3 R.22.a.4.8. to R.16.c.6.6 }	1/1

III LBde RFA

WAR DIARY
or
INTELLIGENCE SUMMARY.
(Erase heading not required.)

Army Form C. 2118.

Instructions regarding War Diaries and Intelligence Summaries are contained in F. S. Regs., Part II. and the Staff Manual respectively. Title pages will be prepared in manuscript.

Place	Date	Hour	Summary of Events and Information	Remarks and references to Appendices
Between POZIERES - OVILLERS.	14.X.16	2.45 P.M.	This brigade fired a barrage in support of attack by 7th Infy Bde 25th divn to establish ourselves on high ground in neighbourhood of STUFF Redoubt from which situation we attained. Our infantry gained objective R.21a.1.2. and R.20d. 90.15. with little loss. Three aeroplane targets engaged between 3-30 and 6 P.M.	3/6
	15.X.16		A quiet day. This aeroplane targets engaged during day. In morning and afternoon all batteries fired with shrapnel on parties of Germans and transport moving in the neighbourhood of MIRAUMONT. Enemy relief apparently was taking place in daylight. Infantry, who could see their targets from front trenches reported our shrapnel fires very effective. Today Corps Commander congratulated the divisional artillery on effective shrapnel hits by us during systematic attack near STUFF Redoubt — slight firing:- this brigade fired 300 rounds (18 Mr) on R22 a.4.6 to R.16 c.8.3. and R22 a.4.6. to R.16 c.6.6. with occasional rounds of H.C. into GRANDCOURT, thirty two fired 60 rounds during night into GRANDCOURT, MIRAUMONT and PETIT MIRAUMONT. — At 6 P.M. very heavy shelling by Germans on trenches near STUFF Redoubt. This brigade retaliated between 8-15 P.M. and 9 P.M. several S.O.S. signals by rocket refracted by all four batteries from SCHWABEN and STUFF Redoubts. At one time batteries (18 prs) were firing 3 rounds per gun a minute. —	3/6
	16.X.16		A lease day; batteries carried out further registrations. (9 aftms 5.9s & 4.2 Hows shells fired for each battery positin) Three German aeroplanes were over battery at one time during afternoon one of which swooped down very low over "A" battery. At night A and B batteries shelled heavily with 8 inch + 5.9 shells. In afternoon Colonel shot to O.C. this Brigade Commander reconnoitred new gun positions for this brigade near MOUQUET farm. Slight firing came on last night.	3/6
	17.X.16		This aeroplane targets during day. Between 5 P.M. and midnight A bty shelled with 8 in + 5.9 shells. Had to cease firing and vacate positions.	3/6

2353 Wt W2544/1454 700,000 5/15 D. D. & L. A.D.S.S./Forms/C. 2118.

111 L Bde RFA

Army Form C. 2118.

WAR DIARY
INTELLIGENCE SUMMARY.
(Erase heading not required.)

Instructions regarding War Diaries and Intelligence Summaries are contained in F.S. Regs. Part II. and the Staff Manual respectively. Title pages will be prepared in manuscript.

Place	Date	Hour	Summary of Events and Information	Remarks and references to Appendices
Between POZIERES and OVILLERS	18.x.16		Quiet day. Battery commander reconnoitred new gun position east of MOUQUET Farm, and work commenced. An aeroplane target engaged during day. Battery ammunition fired at night into GRANDCOURT, MIRAUMONT and PETIT MIRAUMONT.	46
	19.X.16		Nothing to report. All batteries busy digging new gun positions east of MOUQUET Farm. Our target by aeroplane engaged.	46
	20.X.16		Quiet day. Batteries all day engaged in new positions, night firing. 18 hows. on R.16.d + 17.a, 32 rounds during night. —	46
	21.X.16	5 A.M.	Bangalore Torpedoes reported about S.O.S. signal between SCHWABEN and STUFF Redoubts. All guns of the brigade opened fire and continued firing until 5-40 A.M. Germans made attack on SCHWABEN Redoubt but were repulsed leaving 93 prisoners including 4 officers.	46
	13.6 P.M		Wald 75th Divs Bde. no attack by 25th divn on REGINA trench between R.23.a.2.4 and R.30.b.8.5. Attack initially successful whole objective gained and consolidated. 5 officers 619 other ranks returned by this divn. also infantry report our artillery barrage excellent. Night firing night 10.51 imp 31, R.16.c to d + 21.2D — a.4.2D	46
	22.X.16		Quiet day. Batteries preparing new positions east of MOUQUET farm. Slight firing about night.	46
	23.X.16		In morning 3, 18 pr batteries moved into position east of MOUQUET Farm. in R.32.6. No visibility and registration impossible on account of mist and dust but who by German barrage on REGINA trench. Night firing. 18 hr occasional bursts on R.16 + 17. 150 rounds during night. Houtzer on Grandcourt + 40 rounds during night.	46
	24.X.16	6.15 A.M.	Bombardment on GRANDCOURT – S. MIRAUMONT trenches to assist right firing came on east night. No result. — Registration impossible during day + gun battery.	46
	25.X.16	6.15 A.M.	Bombarded GRANDCOURT and S.MIRAUMONT trenches with all batteries. Slight firing on Houtzer. Slight firing on enemy on R.16 + 17. 150 rounds 18 hr barrage on GRAND COURT trench. during night + 40 rds	46

111 Bde RFA

WAR DIARY
INTELLIGENCE SUMMARY

Army Form C. 2118.

Place	Date	Hour	Summary of Events and Information	Remarks and references to Appendices
In the Field Vicinity of TOZIERS to MOUQUET Farm in action	26/10/16	5 A.M.	Germans opened heavy barrage from MOUQUET farm to SCHWABEN REDOUBT. All batteries began firing and continued until 6 A.M.	—
		6-6.15AM	A & D Batteries bombarded BRANDCOURT - SOUTH MIRAUMONT Trench. Two aeroplanes targets engaged during the day. During day each battery fired 130 rounds to harass enemy on BRANDCOURT Trench. Running total to MIRAUMONT 18/11/16. Batteries continued wire cutting on GRANDCOURT Trench.	46.
	27/10/16		Wire cutting by 18 pr on GRANDCOURT Trench continues during day. Colonel E.H.J. Eliote returned from acting C.R.A. Major L.C. MacLellan returns to command of D Bty. Lieut W.R. Sanders wounded in back by shrapnel when observing in HESSIAN Trench on 25th inst.; evacuated to England. Night firing on last night.	46
	28.X.16		No morning bombardment by this brigade. This morning 18 hrs continued wire cutting on GRANDCOURT Trench. Two officers joined brigade from England; Lieut R.R. GYLES posted to B Bty. & Lieut J.W. HORNE to D Bty. Night firing on last night.	46.
	29.X.16		No morning bombardment by this brigade. Two aeroplane targets engaged. No casualties today in brigade, one gunner of A Bty killed by 5.9 shell in gun position. Two gunners wounded at same time. No change in night firing.	46.
	30.X.16		Last night and this morning 2 howitzer batteries moved forward into position S.W. of MOUQUET farm to be able to reach BEAUREGARD Dovecote. Wire cutting and battery registration by 9 a.m. Wire from 18 pr on GRANDCOURT Trench during day to prevent wire being repaired. —	46.
	31.X.16		A quiet day. Batteries 18 hr on wire cutting and inventorying repairs to damage. No bombardment this morning by our guns. Night firing on as on previous four nights.	46.

E Clote Col R.A.
C⁰ 111 Bde R.F.A.

25th. DIVISION

ARTILLERY

111th. BRIGADE   R. F. A.

25th. DIVISIONAL   ARTILLERY

N O V E M B E R   1 9 1 6.

Page 1.

WAR DIARY 111th Brigade RFA
or November
INTELLIGENCE SUMMARY Vol 15

Army Form C. 2118.

Vol 14

Place	Date	Hour	Summary of Events and Information	Remarks and references to Appendices
Same in action line to MOUQUET FARM or east side.	1/11/16		2/B Bty batteries continued firing on GRANDCOURT trench to prevent return being made to work at or remove effective loss today from firing to make roads to days or position, and wagon lines visited by officers. Bty order of B,C & D bell battery in turn in not firing for others, except in case of S.O.S. firing. A. Bty shared today by B & C Bties - It was aeroplane targets engaged during afternoon. Night firing. Shoos on MIRAUMONT, PETIT MIRAUMONT - BOOM RAVINE, 16 hrs on GRANDCOURT and SOUTH MIRAUMONT trenches	4/6.
	2/11/16		with pauses on MIRAUMONT & PETIT MIRAUMONT. Howitzers fired 180 rounds during 24 hours to harass enemy. A quiet day. Night firing as last night. 150 rounds for 18 hrs	4/6.
	3/11/16		Very wet day. 18 hr Bty continued during day, and fire to prevent repair to damaged wire. Seventeen aeroplane targets engaged during day. At midday A, B & C Batteries (in action) were molested by the II Corps Commander. Night firing as usual.	4/6.
	4/11/16 5/11/16		6 right targets by aeroplane engaged during day, at 4 P.M. D Bty bombarded Quarry in L.35.d with fifty rounds H.E and fifty rounds "White Star" lethal shell. Slight firing as usual. Quiet day. Nothing to report. Night firing. 18 hrs 150 rounds during night on GRANDCOURT - S. MIRAUMONT trenches. D. Bty no special task.	4/6. 4/6.
	6/11/16		During day enemy harassed by battlers firing on roads and tracks around MIRAUMONT + PETIT MIRAUMONT. 18 hr fired from time to time on GRANDCOURT trench to prevent repair of wire already cut at 4 P.M. D Bty bombarded Quarry at L.35.d. - a Messer filled with German dugouts - with 58 rounds H.E + 50 rounds lethal shell. Night firing as usual.-	4/6
	7/11/16		Two new officers joined brigade today. 2 Lieut L.B.DAVY. Tintoris Horse and 2 Lieut G.H.HINDS. 18 hrs fired or out inns of GRANDCOURT trench to prevent repair. Visibility bad on account of heavy rain all day. - Slight firing as usual. - At 11 P.M. A Bty fired 50 rds H.E + 50 rds lethal into Quarry at L.35.d.	4/6
	8/11/16		Quiet day. Nothing to report. 2 Lieut G.H.HINDS (Senr. Hons.) joined Bde. posted to A/ Bty. Slight firing as last night.	4.

WAR DIARY or INTELLIGENCE SUMMARY

Army Form C. 2118. Page 2.

111th Brigade RFA
Miraumont
Vol XV

Place	Date	Hour	Summary of Events and Information	Remarks and references to Appendices
Same as return by MOUQUET FARM (on last side)	9/11/16		During day few aeroplane targets engaged. No change in batteries. Have of tds, and this area, shelled continuously with gas shells of various kinds. All batteries were under fire intermittently for most of this period. Result: one man only in brigade sent sick to hospital. Hostile guns complete inactive.	do
"	10/11/16	5.44.5.50 a.m., 6 a.m., 11 a.m.	All batteries of this brigade joined in morning bombardment of enemy line. R.16.b.35.80 to R.18.Ravines. D Bty bombarded Quarry with 50 rounds H.E. 50 rounds lethal shell. During afternoon aero targets from aeroplanes engaged by batteries. All batteries engaged around MIRAUMONT; one working party of infantry engaged. Between 10 PM (Smt Yorks) Infantry raided hostile usually may active in this area. They fired with machine guns or man'd roads. After G.H. HINDS informed attacked to a Bty.	do
"	11/11/16		All batteries joined in morning bombardment from 5.45 – 6 a.m. Visibility bad during afternoon. No change in night firing. 50 rds 18 hr during night on rds Stadium. Flares on Ravines DESIRE Trench.	do
"	12/11/16		Bombarded Quarry, 50 H.E. 50 lethal. Morning bombardment as usual. During afternoon 18 hr battens slowed continuously firing. One regt wounded 6 Bty and two 18 hr guns slightly damaged, by early cow buffers with 5.9 shell. One regt wounded & ambalt fragments and one gun had wheel broken and axle damaged. At night all batteries were very helled by shell fragments and one gun was lay to prevent work.	do
"	13/11/16	7 PM, 6.45 & 6 a.m.	D Battery bombarded Close MIRAUMONT, with 50 H.E. 50 lethal shell. All batteries engaged in connection with attack of 19 Division and other division of further north. 19 Div attack successful and their objective gained. 9.30 to 10 A.M. D battery fired 150 H.E. & 150 lethal shells into the Place MIRAUMONT. During day D Bty fired on dugouts in BOOM Ravine and near GRANDCOURT. Visibility very bad during day on account of heavy mist. Night firing. 18 hrs 200 rounds in brigade to prevent works on GRANDCOURT & DESIRE Trenches. D Bty fired 80 rounds on naval klaxon during night.	do
"	14/11/16		Quiet day. Hostile aeroplane targets engaged by batteries of brigade including some infantry targets. Batteries fires on day two on GRANDCOURT Trench to prevent repair of wire, and 50 rds on all hr trench by 18 hr on dugouts in R.10.L + R.5.c. Night firing. 18hrs 200 rds on cone flares on last night by haut. 80 rds on BOOM Ravine.	do

WAR DIARY or INTELLIGENCE SUMMARY

111 Brigade RFA
November
Vol XV
Army Form C. 2118.
Page 3

Place	Date	Hour	Summary of Events and Information	Remarks and references to Appendices
Guns in action close to MOUQUET FARM (our old trenches)	15/11/16	3 A.M.	D Bty fired 100 lethal shell into Barony at L.35.d.10½. Batteries fired on GRANDCOURT Trench to hold down nepw of wire. Quiet day. Night firing as usual 18/hr 200 rds. How 80 rds.	46
	16/11/16		During day 18 hr battery continued firing on wire of GRANDCOURT and DESIRE Trench to prevent repair. Roads astrides near MIRAUMONT shelled continually by all batteries. Aeroplane targets engaged. No damage in night firing.	46 46
	17/11/16		Quiet day. No aeroplane targets engaged. Enemy wire continued by batteries.	46
	18/11/16	6-10 AM	All batteries fired barrage in support of attack by 18th divn. on DESIRE Trench: six lift only in barrage. 18th divn. whole objective gained. Visibility bad. Batteries continued shooting during day, in bursts. Our last lift at 6.30 A.M. this morning which was charge of morning barrage. Lieut. I. P. RAVALL of B. Bty. wounded by rifle bullet entering his face under right eye, and penetrated to left side of neck. At 6-45 P.M. D Bty fired 378 lethal shells into PLACE, MIRAUMONT.	46
	19/11/16		Lieut W.R. LOADER fires of 6 Bty. wounded. Military roads. Quiet day: nothing to report. Night firing as usual. Sometimes aeroplane targets engaged during afternoon by brigade, and all batteries firing.	46
	20/11/16		Quiet day. Few aeroplane targets engaged. Night firing on GRANDCOURT Trench and roads about MIRAUMONT, and on to front trenches. At 8 P.M. A.B. & C. batteries were shelled by high velocity gun about 6 inch. One Shell landed on B Bty. Dugout dugout, a direct hit. Two gunners killed instantaneously and two wounded.	46
	21/11/16		At 7 A.M. orders were received for brigade to pull out guns from positions, and proceed to wagon lines, preparatory to moving to another area. Batteries continued firing to midday and then commenced to pull out. B Bty handed over positions and guns to battery of 60th Bde. 11th Bde. S.O.A.: A.B. & C. batteries guns all stuck in mud, and at nightfall attempt to move them postponed to next day. Brigade Hqs. handed over to 60th Bde. 11th S.O.A. Mist and fog all day enabled guns to be moved in daylight.	46
Guns in wagonlines near ALBERT	22/11/16	2-30 P.M.	A.B. & C. Batteries pulled out guns during morning and proceeded to wagon lines. SOMME BATTLE completed by II Divn. and Divnl Commander thanked forward Bdes.	46

111 Brigade R.F.A.
November
Vol XIV

WAR DIARY
INTELLIGENCE SUMMARY
(Erase heading not required.)

Army Form C. 2118.

Place	Date	Hour	Summary of Events and Information	Remarks and references to Appendices
On the road to new area.	23/11/16		Brigade left wagon lines near ALBERT at 9.30 A.M. and marched to AMPLIER near DOULLENS. Roads congested with traffic. Brigade ten hours on road.	Apdx. etc.
	24/11/16		Left AMPLIER and marched to LIGNY-SUR-CANCHE west of FRÉVENT.	"
	25/11/16		Left LIGNY-SUR-CANCHE and marched to CONTEVILLE area. A & D Batts at TROIS VAUX. B. Bty at BERVAL. Hd qrs & Bde at HUCLIER.	"
	26/11/16		Bde resting at HUCLIER.	
	27/11/16		Bde still resting at HUCLIER. 111th Batt ceases to exist. A Bty and half B Bty go to 110th Batt; B Bty - half to 112th Batt. D Bty to 112 Batt. Strong accordingly under.	Apdx.

E Clarke Col R A.
O.C. 911 (L) Bde R.F.A.

www.ingramcontent.com/pod-product-compliance
Lightning Source LLC
Chambersburg PA
CBHW081553160426
43191CB00011B/1917